Science 4 Today

Grade 3

by
Margaret Fetty

Frank Schaffer Publications®

Author: Margaret Fetty
Editor: Nathan Hemmelgarn

Frank Schaffer Publications®

Printed in the United States of America. All rights reserved. Limited Reproduction Permission: Permission to duplicate these materials is limited to the person for whom they are purchased. Reproduction for an entire school or school district is unlawful and strictly prohibited. Frank Schaffer Publications is an imprint of School Specialty Publishing. Copyright © 2008 School Specialty Publishing.

Send all inquiries to:
Frank Schaffer Publications
8720 Orion Place
Columbus, Ohio 43240-2111

Science 4 Today—grade 3

ISBN: 0-7682-3523-5

2 3 4 5 6 7 8 9 10 POH 12 11 10 09 08

Table of Contents

Introduction 5
Testing Tips 7
Skills and Concepts 8
Scope and Sequence 11

Science as Inquiry
Week 1: Science Tools 13
Week 2: The Metric System 15
Week 3: The Science Process Skills 17
Week 4: The Scientific Method 19
Week 5: A Good Scientist 21

Physical Science
Week 6: Matter 23
Week 7: Force and Motion 25
Week 8: Machines 27
Week 9: Light 29
Week 10: Heat 31
Week 11: Electricity 33

Life Science
Week 12: Plants 35
Week 13: Animal Needs 37
Week 14: Animal Groups 39
Week 15: Life Cycles 41
Week 16: Ecosystems 43
Week 17: Food Chains 45

Earth and Space Science
Week 18: Rocks 47
Week 19: Land Changes 49

Week 20: Weather 51
Week 21: Water 53
Week 22: Planets 55
Week 23: Earth and the Moon 57

Science and Technology
Week 24: Space Technology 59
Week 25: Energy Technology 61
Week 26: Medical Technology 63
Week 27: Farm Technology 65
Week 28: Computer Technology 67

Science in Personal and Social Perspectives
Week 29: Nutrition 69
Week 30: Exercise 71
Week 31: Safety 73
Week 32: Rain Forest Destruction 75
Week 33: Reduce, Reuse, and Recycle 77
Week 34: Resources 79

History and the Nature of Science
Week 35: Ancient Star Gazers 81
Week 36: Ben Franklin 83
Week 37: Famous Men Scientists 85
Week 38: Famous Women Scientists 87
Week 39: Fossils 89
Week 40: Animal Conservation 91

Answer Key 93

What Is *Science 4 Today*?

Science 4 Today is a comprehensive yet quick and easy-to-use supplement designed to complement any science curriculum. Based on the National Science Education Standards (NSES), forty topics cover essential concepts that third-grade students should understand and know in natural science. During the course of four days, presumably Monday through Thursday, students complete questions and activities focusing on each topic in about ten minutes. On the fifth day, students complete a twenty-minute assessment to practice test-taking skills, including multiple choice, true-false, and short answer.

How Does It work?

Unlike many science programs, *Science 4 Today* adopts the eight major standards outlined by the NSES to ascertain students' science skills. The standards are:

- unifying concepts and processes in science.
- science as inquiry.
- physical science.
- life science.
- Earth and space science.
- science and technology.
- science in personal and social perspectives.
- history and nature of science.

The book supplies forty topics commonly found in the third-grade science curriculum. Educators can choose a topic confident that it will support their unit of study and at least one of the eight standards. The Skills and Concepts chart on pages 8–10 identifies the main concepts for each week to insure that the content aligns with the classroom topic. The Scope and Sequence chart further supports identifying the specific skills following the standards. The answer key, found on pages 93–112, is provided for both daily activities and general assessments.

Published by Frank Schaffer Publications. Copyright protected.   5   0-7682-3523-5   *Science 4 Today*

How Was It Developed?

Science 4 Today was created in response to a need to assess students' understanding of important science concepts. Basals teach the necessary skills, but might not apply them to other overarching standards outlined by the NSES. Moreover, with the increased emphasis on standardized testing, the necessity for experience with test styles and semantics also becomes apparent.

How Can It Be Used?

Science 4 Today can be easily implemented into the daily routine of the classroom, depending on your teaching style. The activities and questions can be written on the board each day, or the whole page can be copied on a transparency and displayed at the appropriate time. It is also possible to copy the weekly page as a blackline master and distribute it at the beginning of each week. Students can complete the activities during attendance or other designated time. After completion, the class can briefly check and discuss the assignment.

What Are the Benefits?

The daily approach of *Science 4 Today* provides reading comprehension practice in science, higher-level thinking exercises, and problem-solving strategies. The pages also target test-taking skills by incorporating the style and syntax of standardized tests. Because of its consistent format, *Science 4 Today* not only offers opportunities for instruction but also serves as an excellent diagnostic tool.

Test-Taking Tips

Short Answer Questions
- Read the directions carefully. Be sure you know what you are expected to do. Ask questions if you do not understand.

- Read the whole question before you answer it. Some questions might have multiple parts.

- If you do not know the answer right away, come back to it after completing the other items.

- Review each question and answer after completing the whole test. Does your answer make sense? Does it answer the whole question?

- Check for spelling, punctuation, and grammar mistakes.

Multiple Choice Questions
- Read the question before looking at the answers. Then, come up with the answer in your head before looking at the choices to avoid confusion.

- Read all the answers before choosing the best answer.

- Eliminate answers that you know are not correct.

- Fill in the whole circle. Do not mark outside the circle.

- Review the questions and your answers after completing the whole test. Your first response is usually correct unless you did not read the question correctly.

True – False Questions
- Read each statement carefully. Look at the key words to understand the statement.

- Look at the qualifying words. Words like *all*, *always*, and *never* often signal a false statement. General words, like *sometimes*, *often*, and *usually*, most likely signal a true statement.

- If any part of the statement is false, the whole statement is false.

Science 4 Today

Week 28 - Pages 67 and 68
Computer Technology
computer
microprocessor
Internet

Science in Personal and Social Perspectives
Week 29 - Pages 69 and 70
Nutrition
food pyramid
balanced diet
nutrients

Week 30 - Pages 71 and 72
Exercise
aerobic exercises
warm-up exercises
cool-down exercises
muscles

Week 31 - Pages 73 and 74
Safety
fire safety
thunderstorm safety
earthquake safety
tornado safety

Week 32 - Pages 75 and 76
Rain Forest Destruction
rain forest
species
slash and burn method
medicines

Week 33 - Pages 77 and 78
Reduce, Reuse, and Recycle
waste
reduce
reuse
recycle

Week 34 - Pages 79 and 80
Resources
resource
renewable resource
nonrenewable resource
inexhaustible resource

History and the Nature of Science
Week 35 - Pages 81 and 82
Ancient Star Gazers
astronomy
stars
constellations

Week 36 - Pages 83 and 84
Ben Franklin
lightning rod
bifocals
odometer

Week 37 - Pages 85 and 86
Famous Male Scientists
George Washington Carver
Thomas Edison
Lewis Latimer

Week 38 - Pages 87 and 88
Famous Female Scientists
Marie Curie
Mae Jemison
Williamina Fleming
Beatrix Potter

Week 39 - Pages 89 and 90
Fossils
fossils
paleontology
dinosaurs

Week 40 - Pages 91 and 92
Animal Conservation
conservation
extinct
endangered
protected

Scope and Sequence

Skills/Concepts	1	2	3	4	5	6	7	8	9	10	11	12	13	14	15	16	17	18	19	20	21	22	23	24	25	26	27	28	29	30	31	32	33	34	35	36	37	38	39	40
Unifying Concepts and Processes in Science																																								
Systems	•	•		•				•			•	•			•	•	•	•			•				•	•		•		•		•			•		•	•		
Order and organization			•	•							•				•		•	•		•	•		•		•				•							•	•	•	•	
Measuring	•	•	•					•																																
Science as Inquiry																																								
Science tools			•					•												•				•																
Science process skills			•																																•	•	•			
Scientific method				•																																•				
Science inquiry					•																		•													•	•		•	
Physical Science																																								
Properties of matter		•				•															•	•			•															
Force and motion							•															•	•		•															
Machines and their uses								•																		•	•													
Properties of light									•														•		•															
Properties of heat										•															•															
Properties of electricity											•														•											•				
Life Science																																								
Plants												•			•							•										•					•			
Animals														•	•							•										•								•
Animal groups														•	•																									
Life cycles															•																									
Ecosystems																•	•															•								•
Food chains																	•																							•
Earth and Space Science																																								
Rocks and minerals																		•																				•	•	

• Indicates Skill or Concept Included

Scope and Sequence

Skills/Concepts	1	2	3	4	5	6	7	8	9	10	11	12	13	14	15	16	17	18	19	20	21	22	23	24	25	26	27	28	29	30	31	32	33	34	35	36	37	38	39	40
Land changes																		•	•													•								
Weather																				•																				
Water cycle						•															•																			
Planets																						•	•																	
Earth and the moon																							•																	
Science and Technology																																								
Natural objects and manmade objects																										•														
Space technology																								•														•		
Energy technology																									•															
Medical technology																										•						•						•		
Farm technology																											•													
Computer technology	•																							•				•										•		
Science in Personal and Social Perspectives																																								
Nutrition																													•											
Exercise																														•										
Safety practices											•																				•									
Rain forest																																•								
Reduce, reuse, and recycle																									•								•							
Resources																																		•						
History and Nature of Science																																								
Astronomy in various cultures																•																			•					
Ben Franklin																																				•				
Famous male scientists																																				•	•			
Famous female scientists																																						•		
Fossils																																							•	
Animal conservation																																								•

0-7682-3523-5 *Science 4 Today* 12 Published by Frank Schaffer Publications. Copyright protected.

Week #1: Science Tools

Name _____

Draw lines to match each tool with what it measures and a unit it measures.

ruler	capacity	grams
thermometer	time	centimeters
balance	length	liters
beaker	temperature	degrees
clock	weight	minutes

Day #1

Read each sentence. Which tool would be used? Write the tool name.

1. Tom measures how tall a plant has grown. _____
2. Maria measures how cold the water is. _____
3. Chen measures how much juice is in an orange. _____
4. Ellis measures how long it takes to run a mile. _____
5. Laurie measures how much mass is in a ball of clay. _____

Day #2

What does a hand lens do?
_____
_____

Name two ways that a scientist could use a hand lens.
_____
_____

Day #3

How are a microscope and telescope alike? How are they different?
_____
_____
_____
_____
_____

Day #4

Published by Frank Schaffer Publications. Copyright protected.   13   0-7682-3523-5   *Science 4 Today*

Name _____ **Week #1:** Science Tools

Assessment # 1

Answer the questions.

Mr. Perez is an ornithologist. He is a scientist who studies birds. Mr. Perez is watching some bluebirds that have built a nest in a nesting box near a meadow. The front of the box opens easily so that Mr. Perez can get close to the birds. What three tools might he use to learn more about the birds? Tell how he would use them.

Tool 1: _____

_____

Tool 2: _____

_____

Tool 3: _____

_____

A computer is another important tool that scientists use. Tell three ways that Mr. Perez could use it in his work with the bluebirds.

Use 1: _____

_____

Use 2: _____

_____

Use 3: _____

_____

Name _____ **Week #2:** The Metric System

Day #1

When people in the United States measure, they use the customary system. Length is measured in inches and feet. Weight is measured in pounds. Capacity uses cups, pints, and gallons. Most other people in the world use the metric system. Every measurement is based on a unit of ten. A meter measures length. There are 100 centimeters in a meter. A liter measures capacity. There are 100 centiliters in a liter. Scientists all over the world, even in the United States, use the metric system when they work.

Why might all scientists use the metric system?

_____

Day #2

Complete the chart with the correct metric units.

Length	Capacity	Weight
1.0 meter	1.0 liter	1.0 gram
10.0 decimeters	_____ deciliters	10.0 decigrams
_____ centimeters	100.0 centiliters	100.0 centigrams
1000.0 millimeters	1000.0 milliliters	_____ milligrams

Day #3

Write the abbreviation for each metric measurement word.

1. liter _____
2. gram _____
3. meter _____
4. centimeter _____
5. milliliter _____
6. kilogram _____
7. millimeter _____
8. decigram _____
9. kilometer _____

Day #4

In the metric system, temperature is measured in degrees Celsius (°C). Water freezes at 0°C and boils at 100°C. The temperature on a hot summer day would be around 30°C.

What is the temperature? Circle the best estimate.

1. a popsicle   0°C   45°C
2. a cup of hot chocolate   15°C   85°C
3. room temperature   20°C   60°F
4. swimming weather   5°C   35°C

Assessment # 2

Look at each metric measurement. Write the name of an object that is about that measurement.

1. 8 centimeters _____
2. 1 meter _____
3. 1 liter _____
4. 100 milliliters _____
5. 1 gram _____
6. 2 kilograms _____

Use a metric ruler. Draw lines to show each length.

7. 30 millimeters

8. 48 millimeters

9. 12 centimeters

10. 7 centimeters

11. Write the temperature shown on the thermometer. Tell what you would do in this weather.

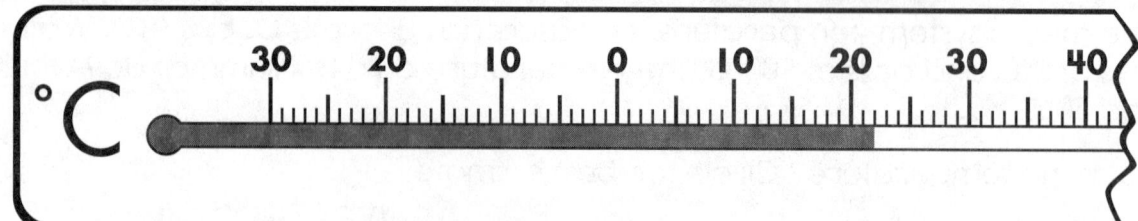

_____
_____

Week # 2: The Metric System

Week #3: The Science Process Skills

Name _____

Day #1

Write a word from the box to identify each skill.

| observe | sequence | classify | compare | predict | infer |

1. Use what you know to make a guess about what will happen _____
2. Use your five senses to learn about the world. _____
3. Tell how things are alike and different. _____
4. Sort objects into groups based on characteristics or qualities _____
5. Use what you know and what you learn to make conclusions _____
6. Put events in time order to show how things change. _____

Day #2

Scientists often measure objects. They record the data and display it in a chart or graph. Inga did an experiment with the weather. It rained for four days. She placed a cup outside. She used a ruler to measure the amount of rain in the cup each night. Look at Inga's data. Make a chart to show the data.

Monday it rained 25 millimeters.
Tuesday it rained 38 millimeters.
Wednesday it rained 2 millimeters.
Thursday it rained 15 millimeters.

Day #3

Make a bar graph to show Inga's weather data.

Day #4

Planning and conducting experiments are two more important process skills. The steps must be done in a certain order for the experiment to work. Number the steps from **1** to **5** to show the correct order for an experiment about digestion.

_____ Count slowly to 30 without chewing the cracker.
_____ Put the cracker in your mouth.
_____ Use a mirror to see what the cracker looks like in your mouth.
_____ Draw a picture of the cracker after counting to 30.
_____ Get a cracker. Draw a picture of it.

Name

Week #3: The Science Process Skills

Assessment # 3

Read the paragraph.

Manny got a good grade on his science test. He decided to put the test on the refrigerator to surprise his mom. He used a magnet to hold the paper on the refrigerator. Manny felt the pull of the magnet as it got close to the steel of the refrigerator. He wondered what else the magnet would stick to. So, he decided to find out. Manny got a dime, paper clip, straight pin, scissors, and aluminum foil. He thought that the dime, pin, and scissors would stick to the magnet, but the others would not. Next, he put the magnet next to each object and watched what happened. If the object stuck to the magnet, he put it in one group. If it didn't, he put the item in a different group. He drew a chart to show his results. Manny guessed that the foil and the dime did not have steel in them because they did not stick to the magnet.

Name at least four science process skills Manny used. Tell how he used the skills.

_____
_____
_____
_____
_____
_____
_____
_____
_____
_____

Name _____   **Week #4:** The Scientific Method

When scientists see a problem, they want to find an answer. They follow steps in a specific order. The steps are called the *scientific method*.

Why do scientists use the scientific method?
_____

What might happen if a scientist did not follow the steps of the scientific method in order?
_____

Day #1

Write numbers **1** to **8** to show the order of the steps in the scientific method.

_____ Observation   _____ Resources

_____ Comparison   _____ Hypothesis

_____ Problem   _____ Presentation

_____ Conclusion   _____ Experimentation

Day #2

Write the name of the step being described.

1. Plan and conduct an investigation or activity.   _____
2. Predict what the results of the investigation will be.   _____
3. Prepare and share a report that shows the data.   _____
4. Draw a conclusion from the results of the investigation. _____

Day #3

Fill in the circle next to the example that is a good hypothesis.

1. (A) Which melts more quickly—ice cream or ice cubes?
   (B) Butterflies are pretty.
   (C) Animals can move seeds.
   (D) Do worms make the soil better?

2. (A) Maple trees are tall.
   (B) Plants need sunlight to grow.
   (C) How much does a cactus grow in one year?
   (D) I think the rose is the best flower.

Day #4

Published by Frank Schaffer Publications. Copyright protected.   0-7682-3523-5 *Science 4 Today*

Assessment # 4

Think about an experiment that you did. Describe what you did and which steps of the scientific method you used.

Week # 4: The Scientific Method

Week #5: A Good Scientist

Name _____

Day #1

Scientists have important characteristics that help them do their best work. Check the characteristics that you think are important for a scientist to have.

_____ curious   _____ patient   _____ creative
_____ watchful   _____ speedy   _____ uninterested
_____ careless   _____ eager   _____ persistent

Choose two characteristics. Tell why they are important qualities for a scientist to have.

_____
_____

Day #2

Communication is another important characteristic of a good scientist. Why must a scientist have this quality?

_____
_____

What are two ways that a scientist might communicate?

_____
_____

Day #3

Read the paragraph. Then, answer the question.

Alexander Graham Bell was a scientist. He became interested in sounds when he was a boy. He studied how people talked as he got older. Bell got an idea of a way to send sound through a wire. He asked Tom Watson, who knew about electricity, to help make a machine that could do this. The men worked on several devices for a year before finding one that worked. They invented the telephone in 1876.

What were two characteristics that made Bell a good scientist? Explain.

_____
_____

Day #4

Read the paragraph. Then, answer the question.

Jane Goodall liked chimpanzees. She went to Africa to learn about them. She spent many years living in a tent in the jungle to watch them. She took careful notes about what she saw. Goodall also photographed and filmed the animals in their natural habitats. She found out many new facts about the chimpanzees and the skills they had. Goodall wrote books and gave talks about her discoveries.

What were two characteristics that made Goodall a good scientist? Explain.

_____
_____

Published by Frank Schaffer Publications. Copyright protected.   21   0-7682-3523-5   *Science 4 Today*

Name

Week #5: A Good Scientist

Assessment # 5

Would you make a good scientist? Why or why not? Write a paragraph that explains at least three characteristics that prove your opinion.

Name _____   Week #6: Matter

Day #1

What is matter?
_____
_____

What are the three states of matter? Describe each state.
_____
_____
_____

Day #2

What are atoms?
_____
_____

Identify each state of matter from the pictures.

1. _____   2. _____   3. _____

Day #3

Read each change to matter. Is it a physical or chemical change? Write **P** for a physical change or **C** for a chemical change.

_____ rust   _____ cook   _____ make a mixture

_____ paint   _____ burn   _____ film process

_____ rip   _____ fold   _____ write on

Day #4

Describe how water changes states.
_____
_____
_____
_____
_____

Name — Week # 6: Matter

Assessment # 6

Answer the questions.

1. Read each item. Write the name of its state.

   desk _____   orange juice _____

   air _____   water vapor _____

   book _____   hot chocolate _____

2. Why does a chair never change shape?

   _____
   _____

3. Imagine that you have two different objects that are the same size. Do these items always have the same mass? Explain.

   _____
   _____

4. Think about making cookies. Describe the physical and chemical changes that take place.

   _____
   _____
   _____

5. Why does a shovel rust if it is left outside in the rain?

   _____
   _____

Week #7: Force and Motion

Name _____

Day #1

What is a force?
_____
_____

Describe what kind of force moves a soccer ball. Then, describe the force that stops it.
_____
_____
_____

Day #2

What is gravity?
_____
_____

Why is it harder to walk up the stairs than to walk down them?
_____
_____
_____

Day #3

Circle the item in each pair that will take more force to move.

| television | book | pan |
| radio | feather | refrigerator |

Why does it take more force to move the items you circled?
_____
_____

Day #4

Choose a word from the box to complete each sentence.

| inertia | friction | speed | lubricant |

1. People often slide on ice because there is no _____ to stop or slow the motion.

2. A car engine needs _____ to keep the parts from rubbing together, which can slow it down.

3. An object stays in motion unless another force acts on because of _____ .

4. The _____ of an object is measured by how fast and how far it moves.

Week #7: Force and Motion

Assessment # 7

Answer the questions.

1. How do you know if a force is working?

   _____
   _____

2. Imagine that you drop a tennis ball and a bag of potatoes at the same time. Explain what will happen and why.

   _____
   _____

3. Would it be easier to ride your bike along a gravel or cement driveway? Explain.

   _____
   _____

Fill in the circle next to the best answer.

4. Two classes are having a tug-of-war. Mr. Jackson's class is pulling Ms. Otto's class closer toward the line. What is happening?

   (A) Mr. Jackson's class is pulling with less force.
   (B) Mrs. Otto's class is pulling with less force.
   (C) Mrs. Otto's class is pulling with more force.
   (D) Both teams are pulling with the same force.

5. Tia and Yukio are racing their bikes to the park. They leave at the exact same time and follow the same path, but Yukio gets to the park first. Why did Yukio get there first?

   (A) Tia had less inertia.   (C) Yukio had more speed.
   (B) Tia had more friction.   (D) Gravity pulled Yukio.

Week #8: Machines

Name _____

Day #1

What is work?
_____

Vince used 3 newtons to move a box 3 meters. Mark used 4 newtons to move the box 2 meters. Who did more work? Explain.
_____
_____

Day #2

What kind of simple machine is each object? Write the name of the machine.

1. seesaw   _____
2. slide   _____
3. fork   _____
4. flag pole   _____
5. screw   _____
6. fishing rod reel _____

Day #3

What is a compound machine?
_____
_____

Name the simple machines in a pair of scissors.
_____
_____

Day #4

Beth is opening a can of paint using a screwdriver. Explain two ways that Beth can use the screwdriver to make different simple machines.
_____
_____
_____
_____
_____

Week #8: Machines

Assessment #8

Fill in the circle next to the best answer.

1. What simple machine is made when a flat surface is set at an angle to another surface?

   A) a screw
   B) an inclined plane
   C) pulley
   D) wheel and axle

2. Which tool is not an example of a lever?

   A) tweezers
   B) nut cracker
   C) hammer
   D) rake

Answer the questions.

3. Shina is pushing on a door, but it does not open. Is she doing work? Explain.

   _____

   _____

4. How do simple machines make work easier?

   _____

   _____

5. Which simple machines are in a wheelbarrow? Tell how each makes work easier.

   _____

   _____

   _____

   _____

   _____

Name _____ **Week # 9:** Light

Complete the following sentences.

1. Light moves in a _____ line.
2. When light bounces off an object and changes direction, the light is being _____.
3. Light that bends as it moves through different kinds of matter is being _____.
4. When light is stopped, the object stopping the light _____ it.

Day #1

Describe how a rainbow forms in the sky.

_____
_____
_____
_____
_____

Day #2

What colors make up white light?

_____
_____

Why is an apple red?

_____
_____

Day #3

Define *transparent*. Name one object that is transparent.

_____

Define *translucent*. Name one object that is translucent.

_____

Define *opaque*. Name one object that is opaque.

_____

Day #4

Published by Frank Schaffer Publications. Copyright protected.   0-7682-3523-5   *Science 4 Today*

Name

Week #9: Light

Assessment #9

Answer the questions.

1. How is a prism like a raindrop?

   _____

   _____

   _____

2. Imagine that you are using a prism to make a rainbow. You shine the colors on yellow paper. What will you see when you look at the paper? Explain.

   _____

   _____

   _____

3. Imagine that you are using a net to scoop a fish out of a tank. The handle of the net looks like it is broken. Why?

   _____

   _____

   _____

4. Why can you see yourself in the surface of a lake?

   _____

   _____

Fill in the circle next to the best answer.

5. A mirror is an example of _____ light.

   (A) reflected   (C) absorbed

   (B) refracted   (D) translucent

Week #10: Heat

Name _____

Day #1

Which are examples of thermal energy? Circle them.

gas	electricity	snowstorm
wind	burning candle	cooking food
sun	lemonade	fireworks

What is heat?

_____
_____

Day #2

Name three examples of thermal energy that you use every day. Tell how each is thermal energy.

_____
_____
_____
_____
_____

Day #3

Describe how thermal energy moves.

_____
_____
_____
_____
_____

Day #4

What is a conductor? Name an example of a conductor.

_____
_____

What is an insulator? Name an example of an insulator.

_____
_____

Name

Week #10: Heat

Assessment #10

Answer the questions.

1. Jessie made a hot fudge sundae. Describe how thermal energy moves in it.

   _____
   _____
   _____
   _____

2. Fran needs a winter coat. Should she buy one that is wool or cotton? Explain.

   _____
   _____
   _____
   _____

3. Is a frying pan an insulator or a conductor? Explain.

   _____
   _____
   _____
   _____

Write *true* or *false*.

4. _____ Thermal heat always moves to a cooler place.

5. _____ Rubbing your hands together can cause thermal heat.

6. _____ Cold particles bump into each other to make thermal heat.

7. _____ The sun does not make thermal heat.

Week #11: Electricity

Name _____

Day #1

What four kinds of energy can electricity make? Write the name of a device that is an example of each.

1. _____
2. _____
3. _____
4. _____

Day #2

What are the three parts of an atom?

_____

An electron has a _____ charge.

A proton has a _____ charge.

A neutron has a _____ charge.

Day #3

Label the diagram to show the parts of a circuit.

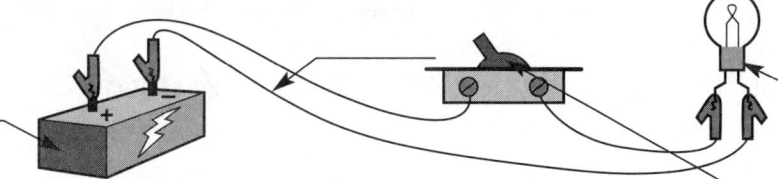

Will the light bulb in the diagram above light? Explain.

_____
_____

Day #4

Write three electric safety rules.

_____
_____
_____
_____
_____

Assessment # 11

Answer the questions.

1. Why is your body a good conductor of electricity?

   _____
   _____

2. Why do workers who repair electric power lines wear rubber gloves instead of glass gloves?

   _____
   _____

3. If you turn on a light switch and the bulb does not glow, what might you guess about the circuit? Explain.

   _____
   _____

4. Explain why you should stay inside during a lightning storm.

   _____
   _____

Darken the circle next to the best answer.

Which of the following is a source in a circuit?

- (A) a battery
- (B) a light bulb
- (C) a switch
- (D) a wire

How does matter move in electricity?

- (A) in a circle
- (B) up and down
- (C) in opposite directions
- (D) in the same direction

Name _____ **Week #12:** Plants

Day #1

What four things do plants need?
_____
_____

Elena bought a plant that she will keep in her bedroom. What must she do to care for it?
_____
_____
_____

Day #2

Label the diagram to show the parts of a plant. Then, tell what each part does.

_____
_____
_____
_____
_____

Day #3

What is a seed?
_____
_____

Tell at least two ways that seeds move.
_____
_____

Day #4

Write *true* or *false*.

1. _____ Photosynthesis is the process in which plants make their own food.
2. _____ Chlorophyll is the energy source that helps plants make food.
3. _____ Sugar is the food plants make.
4. _____ Plants give off carbon dioxide as a waste.

For any sentence that is false, rewrite it to make a true statement.
_____
_____

Assessment # 12

Answer the questions.

Asa does an experiment. She cuts a one-inch circle out of construction paper and paper clips it to the top of a leaf. After one week, she removes the paper circle. What will she see? Explain what has happened.

_____
_____
_____
_____
_____
_____
_____

What do plants need to make food? What is this process called?

_____
_____
_____

Describe three ways that plants are important to people.

_____
_____
_____
_____

Name _____ **Week #13:** Animal Needs

Name four things all animals need.
_____
_____

Choose one animal. Tell how it meets its needs.
_____
_____
_____

Day #1

Animals have body parts that help them get food. Name three animals. Tell how the body parts help them get food.

Animal 1: _____

Animal 2: _____

Animal 3: _____

Day #2

What are three ways that animals protect themselves against predators? Name one animal that uses each method.

Way 1: _____

Way 2: _____

Way 3: _____

Day #3

Write words that complete the sentences.

1. Some animals _____ to places that have warm weather in the winter. One such animal is the _____.

2. Some animals _____ to the cold weather by eating different foods or having body parts that change. The _____ is one of these animals.

3. Another group of animals _____ and sleep through the winter. A _____ does this.

Day #4

Published by Frank Schaffer Publications. Copyright protected. 37 0-7682-3523-5 *Science 4 Today*

Assessment # 13

Answer the questions.

1. How do fish get air?

   _____
   _____

2. The desert kangaroo rat lives in the desert. How might it get water?

   _____
   _____

3. Name two reasons that animals need shelter.

   _____
   _____

4. Tell how a hawk uses two of its body parts to get food.

   _____
   _____

5. Think about a squirrel. Describe three traits that help it live in its forest habitat.

Trait 1: _____
   _____

Trait 2: _____
   _____

Trait 3: _____
   _____

Name   **Week #14:** Animal Groups

There are two main groups of animals in the animal kingdom. What are they?
_____

To which group of animals above do insects belong? Explain.
_____

Choose two insects. Tell two ways they are alike. Then, tell two ways they are different.
_____

Day #1

What are two characteristics of reptiles?
_____
_____

What are two characteristics of amphibians?
_____
_____

Day #2

What are three characteristics of birds?
_____
_____
_____
_____

Day #3

What are the four characteristics of mammals?
_____
_____
_____
_____

Day #4

Published by Frank Schaffer Publications. Copyright protected.   39   0-7682-3523-5   *Science 4 Today*

Name

Week #14: Animal Groups

Assessment # 14

Answer the questions.

1. What are the two main groups of animals? Explain the difference.

   _____
   _____

2. Look at this animal. To which group does it belong? How do you know?

   _____
   _____

3. To which group does a bat belong? Explain.

   _____
   _____

4. A butterfly and bird both have wings and they come from eggs. Why don't they belong to the same group of animals?

   _____
   _____

Fill in the circle next to the best answer.

5. How are reptiles and birds alike?

   Ⓐ They have scales.　　　Ⓒ They have wings.
   Ⓑ They lay eggs.　　　　Ⓓ They have feathers.

6. Which characteristics are not found in mammals?

   Ⓐ give birth to live young　　　　　　Ⓒ have fur
   Ⓑ feed their young milk from their bodies　　Ⓓ swim

0-7682-3523-5　Science 4 Today　　40　　Published by Frank Schaffer Publications. Copyright protected.

Name _____ **Week #15:** Life Cycles

Day #1

What is a life cycle?
_____

Do all living things look like the adult when they begin life? Explain.
_____
_____
_____

Day #2

Write words to tell about how a plant grows.
1. All plants start from a _____.
2. First, a _____ begins to grow.
3. Then, the seed breaks open and a _____ begins to grow under the ground.
4. Soon, the _____ and _____ grow above ground.
5. The plant grows to look like the adult and will grow _____ or _____ that hold the seeds.
6. Finally, the seeds fall to the ground and the _____ begins again.

Day #3

What is metamorphosis?
_____

Write numbers **1** through **5** to show the life cycle of the frog.
_____ Tadpoles swim in the water and breathe with gills.
_____ The tail of the tadpole disappears.
_____ An egg, covered in a jellylike material, stays in the water.
_____ A frog hops out of the water to dry land.
_____ Lungs and legs grow on the tadpole.

Day #4

Describe the life cycle of a human.
_____
_____
_____
_____
_____

Assessment # 15

Label the diagram to show the life cycle of a butterfly. Then, describe the cycle.

_____
_____
_____
_____
_____
_____

Week #16: Ecosystems

Name

Day #1

Draw a line to match each word to its meaning.

ecosystem   the place an animal lives where all its needs can be met
habitat   all the groups of living things that live in a place
population   all the living and nonliving things in a place
environment   a group of one kind of living thing that lives in a place
community   everything that is around a living thing

Name five things that are a part of your classroom environment.
_____

Day #2

Name five living things in a forest ecosystem.
_____
_____

Name five nonliving things in a forest ecosystem.
_____
_____

Day #3

Write the name of the specific ecosystem that correctly completes each sentence.

1. A _____ ecosystem is very dry.
2. It rains almost every day in a _____ _____ ecosystem.
3. Ice and snow cover the land most of the year in the _____ ecosystem.
4. Reefs and colorful fish swim in the salty _____ ecosystem.
5. Water lilies, frogs, and turtles live in a _____ ecosystem.

Day #4

What are three changes, natural or human-made, that might happen in an ecosystem?
_____
_____

How do the above changes affect an ecosystem?
_____

Name **Week #16:** Ecosystems

Assessment # 16

Choose one ecosystem. Draw a picture of it. Include and label at least ten living or nonliving things that are found in that ecosystem.

Week #17: Food Chains

Name

What is a producer?
_____

Where does a producer get its energy?
_____

Why are plants important producers?
_____

Day #1

Describe the three kinds of consumers. Give an example of each.
_____
_____
_____

Where does a consumer get its energy?
_____

Day #2

What is a decomposer? Give an example of two decomposers.
_____
_____

Why are decomposers important in an environment?
_____
_____

Day #3

What is a food chain?
_____

Write **1** to **4** to show the order of consumers and producers in a pond food chain.

_____ fish
_____ plant
_____ duck
_____ insect

Day #4

Published by Frank Schaffer Publications. Copyright protected. 0-7682-3523-5 *Science 4 Today*

Name _____ **Week #17:** Food Chains

Assessment # 17

Complete the activities.

1. Write **P** if the organism is a producer. Write **C** if the organism is a consumer. Write **D** if the organism is a decomposer.

   _____ insect   _____ lettuce   _____ human

   _____ rose   _____ mushroom   _____ tree

   _____ worm   _____ bear   _____ bacteria

2. Describe the food chain below. Use the words in the box in your description.

   | consumer | producer | energy |

   _____
   _____
   _____
   _____

3. What is the most important source of energy? Fill in the circle next to the best answer.

   Ⓐ sunlight
   Ⓑ bacteria
   Ⓒ plants
   Ⓓ animals

Week #18: Rocks

Name _____

Day #1

What is a mineral?
_____
_____

What are the three properties of minerals?
_____
_____

What is the relationship between rocks and minerals?
_____
_____

Day #2

What are the three kinds of rocks? Tell how each is formed?

Category 1: _____
_____

Category 2: _____
_____

Category 3: _____
_____

Day #3

Read each sentence. Tell what kind of rock each hiker finds. Explain how you know.

Leah was hiking in the desert. She picks up a rock. It breaks apart in her hand.
_____

Trevor is walking along a trail through the mountains. He sees a place where some rocks have broken off. There are layers of a hard blue rock showing.
_____

David is in Hawaii hiking up along a trail near a volcano. He sees a black rock filled with holes.
_____

Day #4

Write *true* or *false*.

_____ The rocks on Earth are always changing.

_____ Wind and water break old rocks down, which become sedimentary rock.

_____ Magma cools and forms metamorphic rocks.

_____ Sedimentary rocks can be made into metamorphic rocks.

_____ Heat and pressure help form igneous rocks.

Assessment

Assessment # 18

Answer the questions.

1. How do rocks form and change? Write the names of the kinds of rocks to complete the rock cycle.

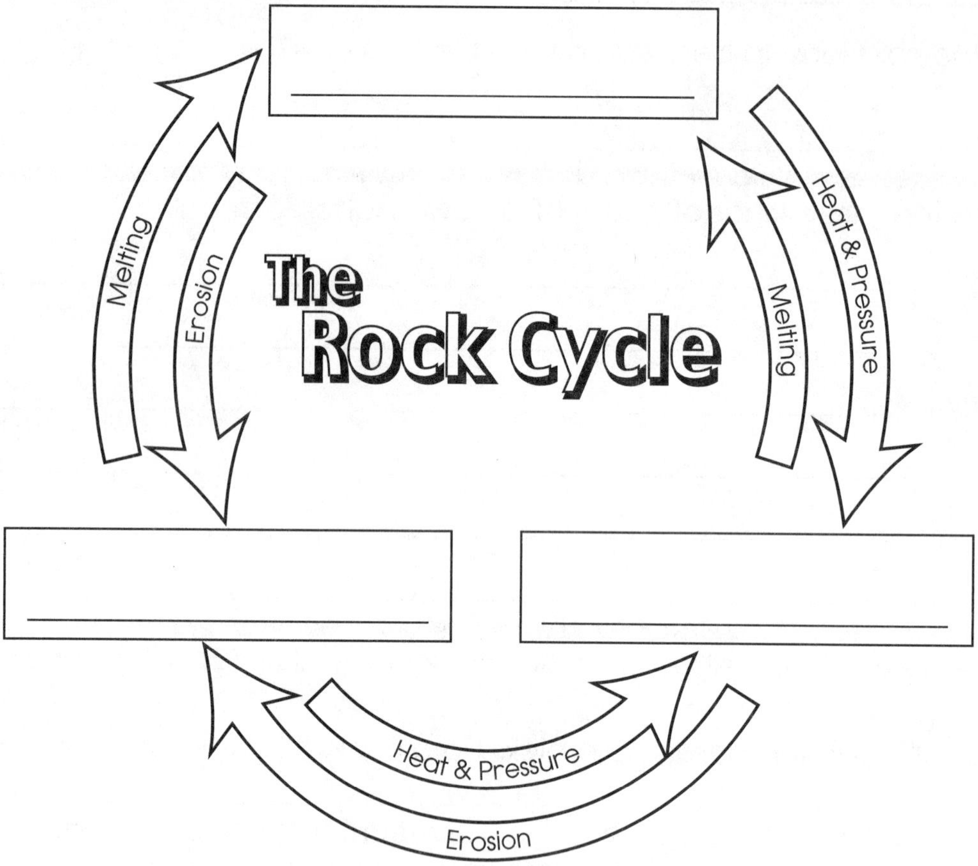
The Rock Cycle
Melting
Erosion
Heat & Pressure
Melting
Heat & Pressure
Erosion

2. What are the three main events in nature that cause rocks to change?

____

____

3. A sculptor is going to make a statue. She is looking at limestone and marble. Which will she most likely choose? Explain.

____

____

____

Week #19: Land Changes

Name

Draw a line from each landform to its meaning.

mountain — flat land rising above the surrounding land
valley — a wide, flat area of land
canyon — a low place between mountains
plain — a piece of land totally surrounded by water
plateau — a deep valley with high sides
island — a very high, pointed pieces of land

Day #1

What is weathering?
_____

What are three weather-related forces that cause weathering?
_____

How do plants cause weathering?
_____

Day #2

How is erosion different from weathering?
_____

Describe two forces that cause erosion.

Force 1: _____
_____

Force 2: _____
_____

Day #3

Read about some changes to the land. Write the name of the event that caused each.

1. The top of the mountain was gone. Red lava poured out of it. Ash filled the sky and drifted in the wind. Smoke rose up into the sky. The whole forest was on fire.
_____

2. The ground began to shake. Suddenly, a large crack formed in the ground. In a nearby house, the windows broke and the building moved off of its cement pad.
_____

Day #4

Assessment # 19

Answer the questions.

1. Which landform would you like to visit. Why?

   _____
   _____

2. A farmer is plowing his fields. Which picture shows the best way to plow the soil to prevent the least amount of erosion? Explain.

   a.   b.

   _____
   _____

Fill in the circle next to the best answer.

3. What is the process where soil is moved from one place to another?

   Ⓐ eruption   Ⓒ erosion
   Ⓑ weathering   Ⓓ orbiting

4. Which of the following can change the ground quickly?

   Ⓐ earthquakes   Ⓒ windstorms
   Ⓑ glaciers   Ⓓ growing plants

5. Which is an example of weathering?

   Ⓐ gravity causing a mudslide
   Ⓑ water moving across the land
   Ⓒ lava flowing down a volcano
   Ⓓ ice freezing in a rock

Name _____

Week #20: Weather

Darken the circle next to the correct answer.

Day #1

1. Which is not a property of weather?
   - Ⓐ land
   - Ⓒ wind
   - Ⓑ temperature
   - Ⓓ precipitation

2. Which of the following affects the weather the most?
   - Ⓐ the clouds
   - Ⓒ the sun
   - Ⓑ the rain
   - Ⓓ the air

Day #2

Write words from the box to name the clouds.

| stratus | cumulus | cirrus | thunderhead |

_____ _____ _____ _____

Day #3

Read the name of each tool. Tell how it helps you understand the weather.

1. thermometer _____

2. anemometer _____

3. rain gauge _____

4. weather map _____

Day #4

What is a meteorologist?
_____
_____

How do air masses affect the weather?
_____
_____

Assessment # 20

Answer the questions.

1. Tell two ways that the weather affects you.

   _____

   _____

   _____

2. It is about 10°C. A warm front is supposed to enter Anna's town on Friday. What kind of weather will Anna most likely see on that day? Explain.

   _____

   _____

3. Suppose you see some cumulous clouds in the sky. What kind of weather are you having?

   _____

Fill in the circle next to the best answer.

4. Which is not a kind of precipitation?

   Ⓐ snow

   Ⓑ rain

   Ⓒ sleet

   Ⓓ clouds

5. How does wind move?

   Ⓐ from cold areas to hot areas

   Ⓑ from hot areas to cold areas

   Ⓒ from areas of high pressure to areas of low pressure

   Ⓓ from areas of low pressure to areas of high pressure

Name   **Week #21:** Water

Day #1
Name five kinds of water features found on Earth?
_____
_____

Why does Earth look mostly blue from space?
_____
_____

Day #2
Name three ways people use water.
_____
_____
_____
_____

Day #3
What are the two main kinds of water? Tell where each is found and why each is important.
_____
_____
_____
_____

Day #4
Draw a line to match each word to its meaning.

water cycle	water in its gas state
evaporation	heat is removed from a gas to change it to water
condensation	heat is added to water to change it to a gas
water vapor	the process where water is removed from the surface of Earth and returned back to Earth

Name

Week #21: Water

Assessment # 21

Look at the diagram. Answer the questions.

1. What does the diagram show?

_____

2. Describe what is happening in the diagram.

_____

_____

_____

_____

_____

Fill in the circle next to the best answer.

3. What causes water to evaporate on Earth?

   Ⓐ the sun   Ⓒ the mountains

   Ⓑ the lakes   Ⓓ the clouds

4. When do clouds form?

   Ⓐ when water vapor heats

   Ⓑ when water vapor condenses

   Ⓒ when the air above water evaporates

   Ⓓ when the air above water condenses

Name   **Week # 22:** Planets

Look at the diagram. Label the planets.

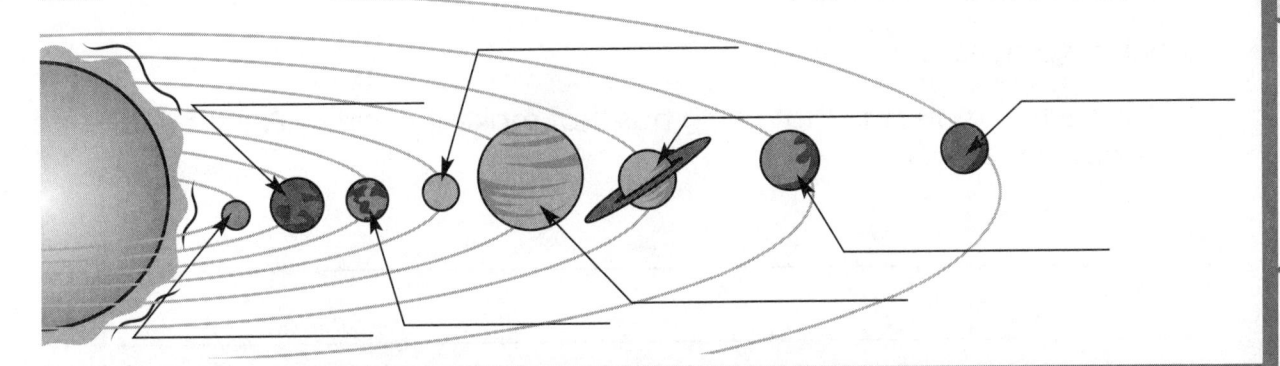

Day #1

Write a word that correctly completes each sentence.

1. The _____ is the center of the solar system.
2. The _____ of the sun is the force that holds the planets in place.
3. All the planets _____ in a circle around the sun.
4. Earth also spins, or _____, on its axis.

Day #2

Write *true* or *false*.

1. _____ Mercury moves the fastest around the sun.
2. _____ Uranus is the hottest planet.
3. _____ Earth is the only planet with living things.
4. _____ Saturn is the only planet that has rings.
5. _____ Uranus is made mostly of gas.

Day #3

What are the names of the inner planets? How are these planets alike?
_____
_____

What are the names of the outer planets? How are these planets alike?
_____
_____

Day #4

Assessment # 22

Answer the questions.

1. Name two materials that Earth has that make it possible for the planet to support life.

   _____

   _____

2. Name two ways that a planet is affected because of its distance from the sun.

   _____

   _____

   _____

3. What would happen to Earth if there was no sun? Explain.

   _____

   _____

   _____

Fill in the circle next to the best answer.

4. Why is the sun's gravity so strong?

   Ⓐ The sun is very hot.   Ⓒ The sun is very big.

   Ⓑ The sun is very bright.   Ⓓ The sun is made of gas.

5. Which planet is an outer planet?

   Ⓐ Earth   Ⓒ Mars

   Ⓑ Mercury   Ⓓ Neptune

Week #23: Earth and the Moon

Day #1

Write *true* or *false*.

1. _____ Earth tilts on it axis.
2. _____ The moon makes its own light.
3. _____ The sun is the largest object in the night sky.
4. _____ The moon revolves around Earth.

For any sentence that is false, rewrite it to make a true statement.

_____

Day #2

Write a word that correctly completes each sentence.

1. We get day and night because Earth _____ around the sun.
2. It takes _____ hours for Earth to make one circle around the sun.
3. When Earth faces away from the sun, that side has _____.
4. When Earth faces toward from the sun, that side has _____.

Day #3

Why does the moon seem to change shape?
_____

About how many days does it take for the moon to make one complete orbit around Earth?
_____

Describe a new moon. Why does it look this way?
_____

Day #4

What are two reasons that Earth has seasons?
_____

Look at the diagram. What season is it in the Northern Hemisphere?

_____

Assessment # 23

Answer the questions.

1. Look at the diagram. What season is it in the Northern Hemisphere?

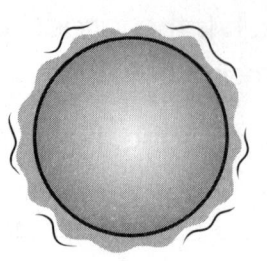

   _____

2. What are two characteristics of the season for the Northern Hemisphere shown above?

   _____
   _____
   _____

3. What would happen if Earth was not tilted?

   _____

Fill in the circle next to the best answer.

4. What are the changes in the moon called?
   - Ⓐ nights
   - Ⓑ years
   - Ⓒ phases
   - Ⓓ seasons

5. What is the moon called when it looks like a half circle?
   - Ⓐ new moon
   - Ⓑ full moon
   - Ⓒ waxing moon
   - Ⓓ crescent moon

Week #24: Space Technology

Name _____

Day #1

A telescope is a tool that many scientists use to study the night sky. It makes objects that are far away look bigger and closer. The first telescopes used curved lenses to pick up the light. Now, the most powerful telescopes use mirrors. Scientists have even sent a telescope into space. It is called the *Hubble Space Telescope*. It stays in the sky above Earth's atmosphere and takes much clearer pictures. The pictures are then sent back to computers on Earth, where scientists can study them.

Why would scientists want to put a telescope in space?

_____

Day #2

Space probes are devices that travel into space without human passengers. They go to a specific place that scientists want to learn more about, including planets and asteroids. Some of the devices do not return to Earth. Others go to a place and pick up items that they bring back for scientists to study. All probes take pictures that are sent back to Earth using radio waves. The most recent probes have landed on Mars.

Scientists often use what they know about Earth to learn about more other planets. Why?

_____

Day #3

The first person traveled into space in 1958. He made one orbit around Earth in less than two hours. Since then, people have many trips into space. Some have even walked on the moon. The spacecrafts from the past could only be used one time. Today, scientists have found a way to use a spacecraft again and again. Crews, composed of men and women astronauts, fly several missions each year. Crewmembers perform different experiments in space. Some missions have been even been made to repair other devices that are in space.

Why would scientists want to repair devices that have been in space?

_____

Day #4

People are living in space! Sixteen countries have combined forces to make this dream a reality. The International Space Station is longer than a football field and as big as a house. When it is complete, it will have five bedrooms. Light from the sun gives the structure energy. The astronauts spend up to six months on it. They study the sun, other planets, and stars. They also do medical experiments to learn about how the body works in space.

What are two problems that scientists living in space might have?

_____

Name

Week #24: Space Technology

Assessment # 24

Answer the questions.

How has technology helped us learn about the solar system?

_____
_____
_____
_____
_____
_____
_____

Would you like to travel in space? Why or why not?

_____
_____
_____
_____
_____
_____
_____
_____

Week #25: Energy Technology

Name _____

Day #1

In some places, the wind is a constant force. Scientists have found a way to convert it into electricity. Giant turbines are built up above the ground. The turbines have blades on them. As the wind blows, it turns the blades and spins the turbine. The turbine powers a generator, which produces electricity.

Why are the turbines built high above the ground?

_____
_____
_____

Day #2

Moving water has energy. People long ago used water energy to turn large rock wheels to grind corn and wheat into flour. People still use water energy today. They build large dams to hold water in lakes. When the water is released, it turns large turbines. The turbines power generators, which produce electric energy. The electricity moves through power lines to light and heat buildings.

Is it possible for all electricity to be powered by water? Why or why not?

_____
_____
_____

Day #3

Solar energy is energy that comes from the sun. Some people use solar energy to heat their houses. Flat, black panels on the roof gather the light. The panels have water-filled tubes inside. The water in these tubes gets hot and travels to a heat exchanger, filled with more water. The heat from the water-filled tubes is transferred to the water in the heat exchanger. The hot water moves through a special heating system to warm a house.

Why are the panels on the roof black?

_____
_____

Day #4

To make nuclear energy, scientists break an atom's nucleus, which creates heat. The heat is converted into steam. Steam powers machines that make electricity. Nuclear energy is good because it does not use fossil fuels, like coal. It does not release pollutants into the air, either. However, the fuel used to split the atoms, uranium, is dangerous once it is used. It must be removed and stored away from living things.

Even with the dangers of nuclear energy, why might many countries continue to build nuclear plants?

_____
_____

Name _____   **Week # 25:** Energy Technology

Assessment # 25

Answer the questions.

1. Why is wind a good source of energy? Why might it be a bad source of energy?

   _____
   _____
   _____

2. Would a homeowner living in Florida or Alaska be more likely to use solar heating? Explain.

   _____
   _____
   _____

3. Other than energy, what are some other benefits of a town building a dam?

   _____
   _____
   _____

4. Which form of energy do you think is the best for people to use? Give two reasons in your explanation.

   _____
   _____
   _____

Name _____   # Week #26: Medical Technology

Day #1

The body has many organs, or body parts, that work together. However, many of these parts are inside and covered up by skin. Sometimes, doctors need to look at these parts if you get sick or hurt. They will use a machine called a *CT machine*. The machine works like a camera. It takes pictures that are like x-rays. A doctor can look at the pictures and quickly see if you are bleeding inside or if something unusual is growing.

What are two reasons that a CT machine is helpful?

_____

_____

Day #2

You eat food and digest it to give you energy. There are many parts that make the process work smoothly. However, sometimes the kidneys do not work. The kidneys are the body parts that remove the wastes from your blood. Luckily, there is a machine to help these people. A dialyzer acts like the kidneys. A nurse attaches some tubes to the sick person. The machine pulls the blood out, cleans the wastes out of it, and returns the blood through another tube. It takes about four hours and must be done three times each week.

How does the dialyzer act like a kidney?

_____

_____

Day #3

Some people can't see things that are close. Others can't see things that are far away. Glasses often correct these problems. Lasers also help people who cannot see things clearly. A laser is a slim, but powerful beam of light. The light makes a cut by burning where it lands. In this case, the beam of light cuts the top layer of the eye. The eye changes shape where it is cut. This kind of surgery is safer than using a knife, and people can use their eyes the next day.

How is a laser like a knife?

_____

_____

Day #4

Jon Comer is a professional skateboarder. He drops into a half-pipe and does many amazing tricks. What is really amazing is that Comer has a prosthetic—an artificial limb—for one leg! Scientists join technology and science to help many people like Comer. The limbs are made of plastic and look real. When joined to the body, muscle movement is changed to electric signals, which makes the artificial limb move.

How do prosthetics help people who are missing limbs?

_____

_____

Name

Week #26: Medical Technology

Assessment # 26

Draw lines to match each word with its meaning.

technology	plastic parts that take the place of missing body parts
prosthetics	a machine that takes pictures of the inside of the body
CT machine	machines and activities that are used to help people
laser	a machine that cleans the blood of wastes
dialyzer	a high-powered beam of light that cuts by burning

Answer the question.

Why is it important that science and technology work together?

_____
_____
_____
_____
_____
_____
_____
_____
_____
_____

Week #27: Farm Technology

Day #1

Long ago, farmers used hand tools, like hoes, to break the soil before they planted seeds. Then, they spread the seeds and harvested the crops by hand. In the 1800s, farmers used iron plows pulled by horses to break the soil. They still spread seed and harvested the crops by hand, though.

How do you think a plow made farming easier?

_____
_____

Day #2

By 1930, farmers used tractors to pull a plow. They also used a harrow to break up big chunks of dirt. Finally, a combine cut and harvested the crop. Where as it took about 32 hours each week in the 1800s to farm an acre, now it took a farmer about 8 hours to do the same work.

How did the new technology help farmers in the 1930s?

_____
_____

Day #3

Today, a farmer can plow a field in about an hour. Moreover, a person with a small farm can buy one tractor and different implements, or tools, to do all the jobs, from plowing to harvesting. Some tractors even have air conditioning.

How might a farmer benefit by buying one tractor and different tools?

_____
_____
_____

Day #4

Is farming easier today than it was a hundred years ago? Explain.

_____
_____
_____
_____

Name

Week # 27: Farm Technology

Assessment # 27

How has technology changed farming? Use the words below in your paragraph.

| plow | tractor | machine | technology |

Week #28: Computer Technology

Day #1

What is a computer?
_____
_____

An abacus was a tool that merchants used to calculate numbers in ancient China. Many people think it is the first computer. Why?
_____
_____

Day #2

Draw a line to match each word with its meaning.

monitor   a program that makes the computer work
keyboard   the network that links computers all over the world
file   the part on which people input the information
microprocessor   the part that does the computing
Internet   the smallest unit in which information is stored
software   the part where people see the information
memory chip   the part that stores all the information

Day #3

Name four ways that people use a computer to communicate.
_____
_____
_____
_____

Day #4

Why is a digital camera a kind of computer?
_____
_____
_____
_____

Week #28: Computer Technology

Name

Assessment

Assessment # 28

How have computers changed society? Use the words from the box in your paragraph.

| work | play | learn | communicate |

Name **Week #29:** Nutrition

Day #1

Label the food pyramid.

Why is there a person walking up steps on the pyramid?

_____
_____
_____
_____

Day #2

What did you eat during your last meal? Write the name of each food. Tell which food group it is from.

_____
_____
_____
_____

Day #3

What is a balanced diet?

_____
_____

Why should you eat a balanced diet?

_____
_____

Day #4

Draw a line to match the food with its nutrient.

fish	vitamin A
carrots	vitamin C
milk	iron
spinach	protein
bread	carbohydrate
oranges	calcium

Assessment # 29

Answer the questions.

1. Not all people should eat the same amounts of food. For example, a two year-old girl will not need to eat as many servings of fruit as an eight-year old girl. Explain why.

   _____
   _____

2. Why is it important to eat foods from different food groups?

   _____
   _____

3. What happens to a person who eats foods that have too many fats or sugars?

   _____
   _____

4. Lana is having some friends over after school. What is a nutritious snack that she might share with her friends?

   _____

Fill in the circle next to the best answer

5. What do proteins help the body?

   Ⓐ They help it grow.　　　Ⓒ They keep the body warm.
   Ⓑ They build muscles.　　Ⓓ They help you see.

6. Which food is part of the grain group?

   Ⓐ peas　　　Ⓒ nuts
   Ⓑ yogurt　　Ⓓ noodles

Name _____   **Week #30:** Exercise

Day #1

Name two ways that exercise helps your body.
_____
_____

What might happen if you do not exercise your muscles?
_____
_____
_____

Day #2

How does your body change when you do warm-up exercises?
_____
_____
_____

Name two reasons that you should warm-up before exercising.
_____
_____
_____

Day #3

What is an aerobic exercise?
_____

What two parts of your body work harder during aerobic exercises?
_____

Write **A** on the line if the activity gives you an aerobic workout.

_____ jumping rope   _____ skating   _____ running
_____ watching TV   _____ playing cards   _____ tossing a ball
_____ swimming   _____ biking   _____ dancing

Day #4

Why should you give your body time to cool down after exercising?
_____
_____
_____

How does stretching after exercising help you muscles?
_____
_____
_____

Name　　　　　　　　　　　　　　　　　　　**Week #30:** Exercise

Assessment # 30

Write *true* or *false*.

1. _____ When you warm-up, you should run very fast.
2. _____ Warming-up will prevent muscles from getting hurt.
3. _____ You should never bounce when you stretch.
4. _____ Exercising will help control stress.
5. _____ A person should do some sort of aerobic activity every day.

Answer the questions.

6. Why is it good to do many different activities and exercises?

   _____

   _____

7. Jan stretched for five minutes. Then, she jumped rope with her friends for thirty minutes. She sat down right away to eat an apple. Did Jan do a correct workout? Explain.

   _____

   _____

Fill in the circle next to the best answer.

8. How does aerobic exercise help your lungs?

   (A) They hold more air.　　(C) You can smell better.
   (B) You can breathe faster.　(D) All of the above.

9. How does exercise help your body?

   (A) You can play longer.　　(C) You can move more easily.
   (B) You are stronger.　　　(D) All of the above.

Week #31: Safety

Name _____

Unscramble the letters in bold to complete the fire safety rules.

1. Put smoke **srcotdeet** near the bedrooms. _____
2. Make a plan to **speeca** from every room in the house. _____
3. Choose a place where everyone should meet **duostie**. _____
4. Keep a fire **stuigehrnixe** on each floor in the house. _____
5. If your **selocht** catch on fire, you should stop, drop, and roll. _____

Day #1

Think about thunderstorm safety. Write *true* or *false*.

1. _____ Stay away from glass windows and doors.
2. _____ Stand under a tree if there is lightning.
3. _____ Stay away from water.
4. _____ If you cannot reach shelter, get down on your knees and tuck your head.
5. _____ Stay talking on the phone with an adult.

Day #2

If you are in a building, what should you do during an earthquake?
_____
_____

If you are outside, what should you do during an earthquake?
_____
_____

Day #3

Write words to correctly complete the tornado safety rules.

1. Move to a room that does not have _____.
2. If you are outside and cannot reach shelter, move to a _____.
3. Listen to weather _____ on the TV or radio.
4. Stay put until the danger is _____.

Day #4

Published by Frank Schaffer Publications. Copyright protected.   0-7682-3523-5 *Science 4 Today*

Name **Week #31:** Safety

Assessment # 31

Answer the questions.

1. Why is it important to move away from glass windows and doors during earthquakes and tornadoes?

   _____
   _____

2. Why should you not stand under a tree during a thunderstorm?

   _____
   _____

3. How do smoke detectors keep people safe during fires?

   _____
   _____

4. Why is it important to learn and practice safety rules?

   _____
   _____

5. The numbers 911 and 311 are important numbers to know. What are they used for? Identify a situation when you would use each number.

   _____
   _____
   _____
   _____

Week #32: Rain Forest Destruction

Day #1

More than half of all plants and animal species in the world live in the rain forest. Scientists believe that millions more exist, but have not yet been discovered. However, in the last fifty years, nearly half of the rain forests have been destroyed.

Why might scientists be concerned about the loss of the rain forests?

_____
_____
_____

Day #2

The rain forest is of great interest to many companies. Loggers cut large areas of trees to harvest the wood for a variety of products. Miners strip the land of trees to dig out minerals. The land is left bare once the companies take what they want.

Is it a good idea to leave the land bare? Explain.

_____
_____
_____

Day #3

People have lived in the rain forest for thousands of years. Each year, they burn parts of forest so they can grow crops. So many of them use the slash and burn method that huge clouds of smoke are carried to other continents. Moreover, rain forest soil is thin and does not have many nutrients. After farming the land for several years, the soil no longer grows healthy plants. The people clear more trees to make new fields.

Tell two ways that the slash and burn method is harmful.

_____
_____

Day #4

The native people use the plants in the rain forest for medicines. Drug companies are working with them to find out which plants they use to cure different illnesses. Then, scientists research how to use the plants to make new medicines. For example, the rosy periwinkle, a flower grown in the Madagascar rain forest, is now used to make a drug that helps cancer patients.

How is the relationship between drug companies and native people a positive event?

_____
_____

Name _____

Week #32: Rain Forest Destruction

Assessment # 32

Fill in the circle next to the best answer.

1. What is the slash and burn method?

    Ⓐ logging companies dig out minerals

    Ⓑ workers find and cook food

    Ⓒ native people clear land to grow crops

    Ⓓ logging companies cut down trees

2. Why is it important to work with the native people living in a rain forest?

    Ⓐ They know about the plants and animals.

    Ⓑ They want to sell their land.

    Ⓒ They don't want strangers in the rain forest.

    Ⓓ They want to make money logging.

Write a paragraph telling three reasons why the rain forest is important.

_____
_____
_____
_____
_____
_____
_____
_____
_____

Week #33: Reduce, Reuse, and Recycle

Day #1

Which kind of trash is thrown out the most?
_____

What are three examples of this kind of trash that you throw out?
_____
_____
_____

Paper 40%
Yard Trimmings 18%
Metals 8%
Plastics 8%
Food Scraps 7%
Glass 7%
Other 12% (rubber, leather, cloth, wood, misc.)

Day #2

Draw a line to match each word with its meaning.

waste   to make something new out of something old

reduce   to use less of something

reuse   to find a new use for something

recycle   something that is thrown out

Day #3

Kristi has a shoebox. What are two ways that she can reuse it?
_____
_____

Baytown has a water shortage. What are two ways people can reduce the amount of water they use?
_____
_____

Day #4

Write a word to complete each sentence.

1. Save _____ by turning off the faucet when you brush your teeth.
2. Save _____ by turning off lights that are not being used.
3. Give _____ you grow out of to someone who can wear them.
4. Use dishes instead of _____ plates when you eat.
5. Recycle your soda cans because the _____ can be used to make new products.

Name: _____ **Week #33:** Reduce, Reuse, and Recycle

Assessment # 33

Fill in the circle next to the best answer:

1. Which product comes from trees?
   - (A) plastic
   - (B) glass
   - (C) paper
   - (D) aluminum

2. Which is not a use for recycled glass?
   - (A) roads
   - (B) bowls
   - (C) earrings
   - (D) shoebox

Answer the questions:

3. Give an example telling how you can help Earth.

Reduce: _____
_____

Reuse: _____
_____

Recycle: _____
_____

4. Why is it important to reduce, recycle, and reuse items?
_____
_____
_____
_____

Week #34: Resources

Name _____

Day #1

What is a resource?
_____
_____

Write **R** beside things each item that is a resource.

____ air   ____ corn   ____ water
____ cow   ____ oil   ____ coal
____ shirt ____ electricity ____ paper

Day #2

Look at each picture. Tell why it is a resource.

_____
_____
_____

_____
_____
_____

Day #3

What is a renewable resource? Give two examples.
_____
_____

What is an inexhaustible resource? Give two examples.
_____
_____
_____

Day #4

Where are most nonrenewable resources found?
_____

Should nonrenewable resources be used carefully? Explain.
_____
_____
_____

Week #34: Resources

Assessment # 34

Answer the questions.

1. Look at the picture. How is it a resource?

   _____
   _____
   _____
   _____

2. Is it important to care for inexhaustible resources? Give an example in your explanation.

   _____
   _____

3. How does a lumber company make sure that a tree is a renewable resource?

   _____
   _____

Fill in the circle next to the best answer:

4. What kind of resources are plants and animals?

   Ⓐ exhaustible   Ⓒ renewable
   Ⓑ inexhaustible   Ⓓ nonrenewable

5. Which is not an example of a nonrenewable resource?

   Ⓐ coal   Ⓒ oil
   Ⓑ iron   Ⓓ water

Week #35: Ancient Star Gazers

Day #1

Draw a line to match each word with its meaning.

astronomy	a ball of burning gas
astronomer	a group of stars that forms a pattern
constellation	the study of objects in the solar system
star	a tool that makes far away objects bigger and closer
telescope	a person who studies objects in the solar system

Day #2

Ancient cultures that lived long ago did not have tools to observe the sky, so they only used their eyes to see the brightest objects. Some ancient people in Greece and Rome recognized that some stars formed patterns, or constellations. They named the constellation for activities and animals they knew, like a bear, dog, crab, and hunter. These ancient star gazers learned to predict seasons based on the movement of the stars.

What science processes did the Greeks and Romans use to study the stars?
_____
_____

Day #3

The Egyptians lived along the Nile River. Each year the river flooded. The people looked forward to this time, because the flooding brought rich soil that helped them grow healthy crops. For a while, they never knew exactly when the flood would begin. However, they soon discovered that one special star rose ahead of the sun each year. This was the sign that let them know the floods would follow.

How did the Egyptians use the stars in their daily life?
_____
_____

Day #4

Sailors moved around the world on the ocean. They were often far away from land. They needed the stars in the sky to help them navigate, or move in a direction, so they could get back home. One star never moved in the sky. This was the North Star. It always showed which way was north. Sailors also used a map that showed all the stars to guide them.

How might using stars as a guide be a problem?
_____
_____

Week #35: Ancient Star Gazers

Assessment # 35

Answer the questions.

1. What were two reasons that ancient people were interested in the stars?

   _____
   _____
   _____

2. How did observing help the ancient people learn about the stars?

   _____
   _____
   _____

3. Think about how the Greeks and Romans named constellations. What name would you give to a star pattern? Explain.

   _____
   _____
   _____

Write *true* or *false*.

4. _____ Sailors used the bear star to know which way to sail.

5. _____ Egyptians watched for the bright star that would rise before the sun.

6. _____ The flooding of the Nile River was a clue that it was time to plant crops.

7. _____ The Greeks and Romans named many constellations.

Week #36: Ben Franklin

Name _____

Day #1

If you hear the name Ben Franklin, you probably think about a man who helped shape the government of the United States. However, Franklin was also a scientist. He was very curious. If Franklin saw a problem, he wanted to find a solution. Franklin often did experiments to find out more about his ideas. He wrote careful notes about what he did, what he saw, and what happened. You can still read many of Franklin's notes today.

Was Franklin a good scientist? Explain.
_____
_____

Day #2

Ben Franklin had two pairs of glasses. One pair was used to see far away objects. The other pair was used to see nearby objects. Franklin got tired of switching glasses. He found a way to use one pair of glasses. He had the lenses from each pair of glasses cut in half and put into one frame. They were a success. Ben Franklin had invented bifocals.

What problem did Franklin solve?
_____
_____

Day #3

Ben Franklin is well known for his kite experiment. He believed that lightning was a kind of electric current. To test his idea, he tied a metal key to the end of a kite. He flew the kite in a storm. The lightning hit the kite and traveled down the string to the key. A spark jumped to Franklin's hand. The experiment led to the invention of the lightning rod.

What might have been Franklin's hypotheses about lightning?
_____
_____

Day #4

Ben Franklin organized the first post office system. He wanted to plan the best routes to deliver the mail. However, he did not have a way to measure the distance between the houses and businesses. Franklin created an odometer to calculate how far the mail would have to be taken. He attached the odometer to his carriage and rode around town.

What did the odometer do?
_____
_____

Name   **Week #36:** Ben Franklin

Assessment # 36

Fill in the circle next to the best answer.

1. Which device did Franklin not invent?

    (A) odometer   (C) lightning rod

    (B) eye glasses   (D) bifocals

2. Which characteristic best describes Franklin's work as a scientist?

    (A) careful   (C) changing

    (B) careless   (D) confused

Answer the questions.

3. How did inventing the odometer solve a problem?

    _____
    _____

4. Think about the kite experiment. Why do you think that Franklin chose to use a kite and key?

    _____
    _____
    _____

5. Were Ben Franklin's inventions useful? Explain.

    _____
    _____
    _____
    _____

Week #37: Famous Men Scientists

Name _____

Day #1

What do shaving cream, mayonnaise, peanut butter, and cherry punch have in common? George Washington Carver! He was an inventor and scientist who worked with plants. By the 1900s, the soil in the south did not have many nutrients, and it did not hold water well. The cotton plants that had been grown for years had hurt the soil. Carver found that planting peanuts and sweet potatoes helped the soil.

How did planting peanuts and sweet potatoes help the soil?

_____
_____

Day #2

Thomas Edison had over 1,000 patents with his name on it. A patent gives a person or company who has an idea the right to be the only one who can use, make, or sell things with the idea. Edison spent many years learning about electricity and sound. One of his most well-known patents was received for the thread inside a light bulb. It made using lights in a house safe and useful. It was not too expensive, either.

Why would a scientist want to patent an idea?

_____
_____

Day #3

Putting lights in one house was easy. Yet Edison needed to find a way to get lights into every house. He needed to invent a system to link electricity to each house and business in a town. With more experiments, Edison invented parallel circuits, an underground conductor network, safety fuses, and off-on switches.

What problem did Edison have with lights?

_____
_____

Day #4

Thomas Edison may have invented an electric system, but it was Lewis Latimer who made improvements to the light bulb that really made it safe. Edison's light bulb only pushed into a socket. The bulb could easily fall out if the lamp tipped. Latimer invented a bottom that had threads. It could be screwed into the socket. Now the electric lamp was really safe.

Did adding screws to the bottom of the bulb make it safer? Explain.

_____
_____

Week #37: Famous Men Scientists

Assessment # 37

Write *true* or *false*.

1. _____ Thomas Edison invented the light bulb.
2. _____ Sweet potatoes can add nutrients to soil.
3. _____ Peanuts can be used to make shaving cream.
4. _____ Lewis Latimer improved the light bulb.
5. _____ Latimer's bulb was improved using a simple machine.

Answer the questions.

6. How did communication help improve the light bulb?

_____
_____
_____

7. Why did Thomas Edison need to invent a system for lights?

_____
_____
_____
_____

8. George Washington Carver invented over 100 uses for peanuts alone. Why do you think he did this?

_____
_____
_____

Week #38: Famous Women Scientists

Day #1

Marie Curie is one of the most famous female scientists. She won many awards, including the Nobel Peace Prize two times. She was a chemist and physicist who studied radioactive minerals, nonliving things in nature that gave off energy in the form of rays. Through her work, Curie discovered two new elements and developed the use of x-rays.

Why do you think Curie is famous?

_____
_____

Day #2

As a child, Mae Jemison liked science and math. She learned about medicine in college. When she graduated, she wanted to help people. She worked in several countries that did not have good health care. Jemison returned to the United Sates and became an astronaut. She was the first African-American woman to travel into space. When Jemison left the space program, she continued to help people in other countries by setting set up a satellite system that improved health care.

How could a satellite system help people in far away places?

_____
_____

Day #3

Williamina Fleming never went to school. She began working for an astronomy professor as a maid. The professor saw that Fleming was observant and wise. He asked Fleming to work for him. Fleming watched and listened to the professor. She began to study the stars. Fleming created a system to organize, or classify, stars. In one year alone, Fleming discovered 222 stars! Fleming also identified a white star, which, from its color, showed that the star was about to die.

Why is having a system to classify stars important?

_____
_____

Day #4

You probably know the name Beatrix Potter. She wrote and illustrated "The Tale of Peter Rabbit." However, did you know that Potter was also a botanist, or a plant scientist? She studied fungi, living things that live on dead plant and animal matter. She collected samples of many different fungi and then cut them open to look inside. Then she would paint pictures filled with details to show what they looked like. Amazingly, Potter made over 300 pictures of mushrooms alone.

How might Potter's pictures help other scientists?

_____
_____

Week #38: Famous Women Scientists

Assessment # 38

Draw a line to match each word with its meaning.

1. astronomer   a person who studies plants
2. physicist   a person who studies matter and energy
3. chemist   a person who studies stars
4. botanist   a person who studies materials and how they work together when joined

Answer the questions.

5. How might an outside interest help a scientist? Give an example.

_____

_____

_____

6. How do many different people from around the world benefit from work scientists do? Give an example.

_____

_____

_____

Fill in the circle next to the best answer.

7. Which activities was Beatrix Potter interested in?

   Ⓐ botany and writing   Ⓒ astronomy and writing
   Ⓑ chemistry and botany   Ⓓ physics and chemistry

8. Why is Mae Jemison famous?

   Ⓐ She won two Pulitzer Prizes.
   Ⓑ She created a system to classify stars.
   Ⓒ She was the first African-American woman in space.
   Ⓓ She discovered the x-ray.

Name

Week #39: Fossils

Day #1

Draw a line to match each word with its meaning.

fossil — the shape of a living thing left as an imprint
paleontology — a kind of animal that lived long ago
mold — the study of fossils
cast — something left over from a living thing that died long ago
dinosaur — the shape of a living thing made when mud or minerals fill a space

Day #2

Write numbers 1 through 5 to show how a fossil is made.

_____ The soft parts rot.

_____ Layers of small rocks, sand, and mud cover the organism.

_____ The plant or animal dies.

_____ A print of the organism remains in the rock.

_____ The pressure of the layers of sediment forms rock.

Day #3

How do we know that dinosaurs lived on Earth?
_____
_____

Why must a paleontologist work carefully when digging up fossils?
_____
_____

Day #4

Professor Ray has two fossil teeth. One is long and pointed. The other is wide and flat. List two facts that Professor Ray can make about these teeth. Explain each fact.

Fact 1: _____
_____

Fact 2: _____
_____

Name _____ **Week #39:** Fossils

Assessment # 39

Answer the questions.

1. Why are most fossils found in sedimentary rocks?

   _____

   _____

2. What is the difference in a cast and a mold fossil?

   _____

   _____

   _____

3. How might knowing about plants and animals living today help scientists learn about organisms that lived long ago?

   _____

   _____

   _____

4. Identify three tools a paleontologist needs to help dig fossils and explain their uses.

   Tool 1: _____

   _____

   Tool 2: _____

   _____

   Tool 3: _____

   _____

Week #40: Animal Conservation

Name _____

Draw a line to match each word to its meaning.

conservation — there is only a small number of this living thing

extinct — a place where the habitat of a living thing is kept safe

endangered — a group of living things that is being kept safe by laws

protected — every one of this kind of living thing has died

refuge — to keep the living things on Earth safe

Day #1

Dinosaurs lived long ago. How do we know that these animals existed?

_____

Why do scientists think that all the dinosaurs died?

_____
_____
_____

Day #2

Bluebirds live in holes they find. The holes may be in trees or in fence posts. People started clearing the land to make roads, buildings, and farms. The bluebird population got smaller. Soon, the bird was added to the endangered list.

Think about what animals need. What did the bluebird not have?

_____

What did people do that caused the bluebird population to get smaller?

_____

Day #3

People worried that bluebirds would become extinct. They began to help the birds. People all over the United States built special boxes that the birds could live in. They nailed the boxes to trees beside meadows. Now the bluebird population is growing. The bluebirds have been removed from the endangered list in some states.

Describe two human activities that helped the bluebirds.

_____
_____

Day #4

Published by Frank Schaffer Publications. Copyright protected.   91   0-7682-3523-5   *Science 4 Today*

Week #40: Animal Conservation

Assessment # 40

Read the selection. Then, answer the questions.

The bald eagle is the national symbol of the United States. At one time, many of these birds flew in the sky. Then, farmers began using chemicals to kill insects. Fish and other small animals ate the insects. The chemical was in those animals. The eagles then ate those animals. They too had the chemical in their bodies. They began laying eggs with thin shells. When the parents sat on the eggs, the eggs cracked. Few eagles were born. The bald eagle was added to the endangered list.

Scientists were puzzled. The chemicals were not used near the eagles. They worked to solve the problem. Now, those chemicals are not used. People are working to make sure the eagles have everything they need so their population will grow.

1. How did people harm the eagles?

   _____

   _____

2. How did knowing about a food chain help scientists discover the problem with eagles?

   _____

   _____

3. How did people help the eagles?

   _____

   _____

4. Why is it important to understand the balance of nature?

   _____

   _____

   _____

Answer Key

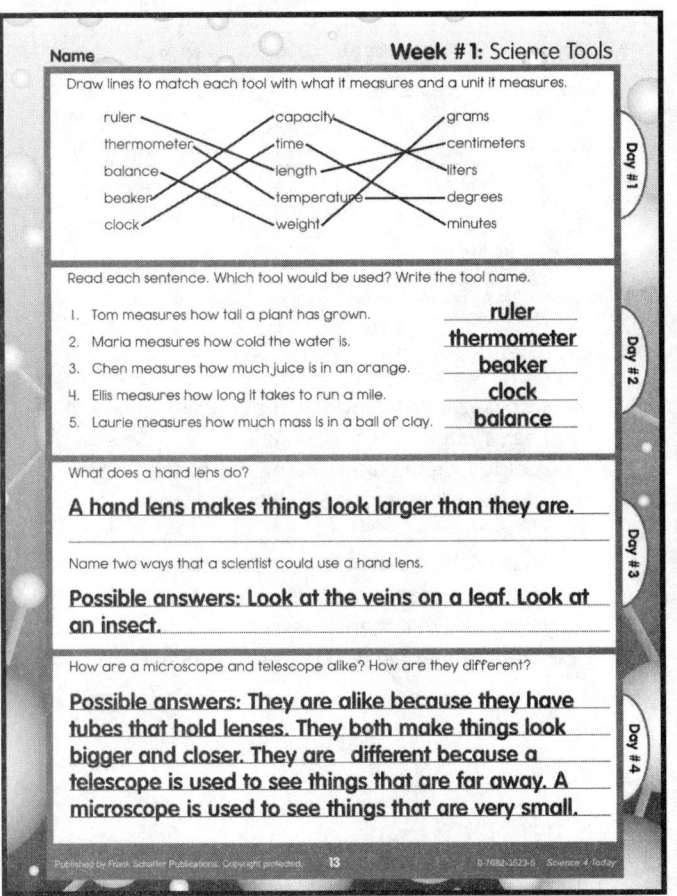

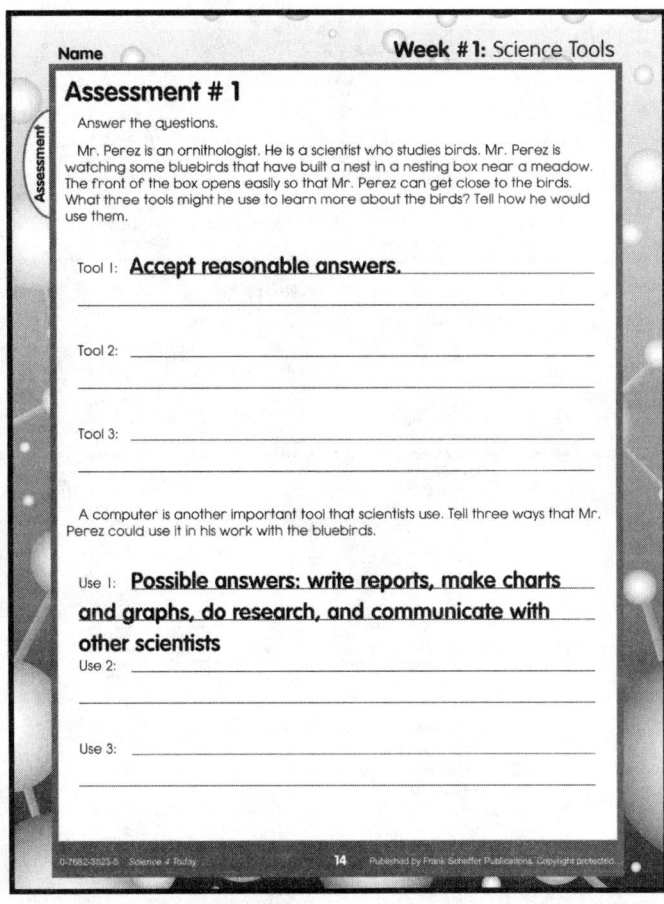

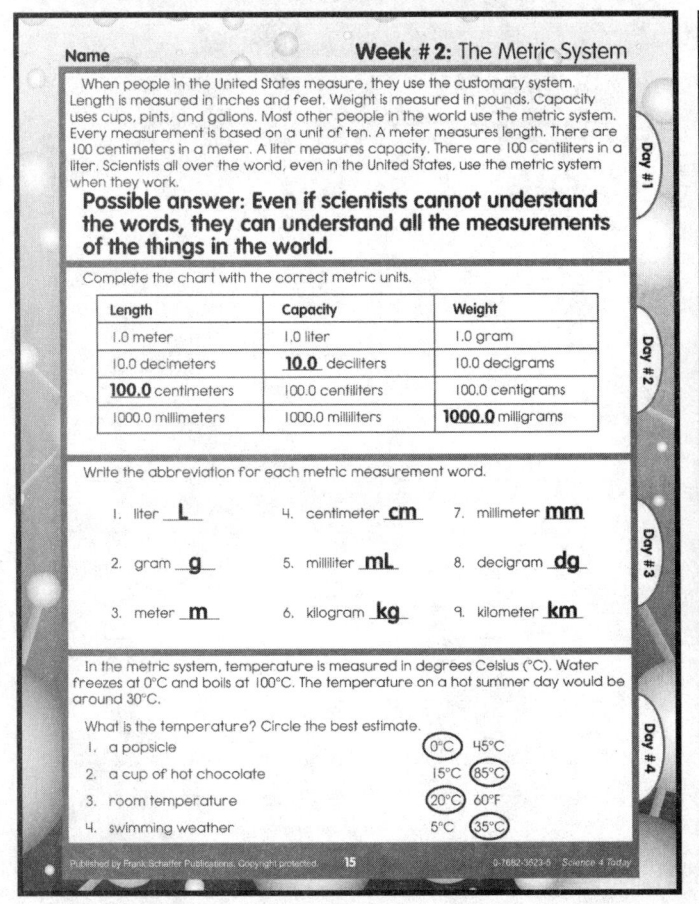

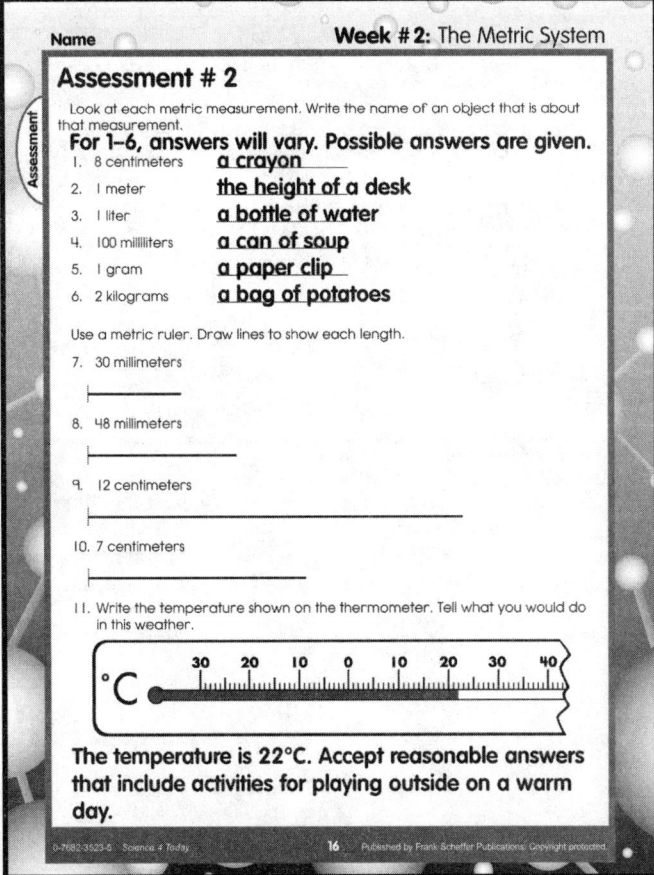

Week #1: Science Tools — Day #1

Draw lines to match each tool with what it measures and a unit it measures.

- ruler — length — centimeters
- thermometer — temperature — degrees
- balance — weight — grams
- beaker — capacity — liters
- clock — time — minutes

Day #2

Read each sentence. Which tool would be used? Write the tool name.

1. Tom measures how tall a plant has grown. **ruler**
2. Maria measures how cold the water is. **thermometer**
3. Chen measures how much juice is in an orange. **beaker**
4. Ellis measures how long it takes to run a mile. **clock**
5. Laurie measures how much mass is in a ball of clay. **balance**

Day #3

What does a hand lens do?

A hand lens makes things look larger than they are.

Name two ways that a scientist could use a hand lens.

Possible answers: Look at the veins on a leaf. Look at an insect.

Day #4

How are a microscope and telescope alike? How are they different?

Possible answers: They are alike because they have tubes that hold lenses. They both make things look bigger and closer. They are different because a telescope is used to see things that are far away. A microscope is used to see things that are very small.

Week #1: Science Tools — Assessment #1

Answer the questions.

Mr. Perez is an ornithologist. He is a scientist who studies birds. Mr. Perez is watching some bluebirds that have built a nest in a nesting box near a meadow. The front of the box opens easily so that Mr. Perez can get close to the birds. What three tools might he use to learn more about the birds? Tell how he would use them.

Tool 1: **Accept reasonable answers.**

Tool 2:

Tool 3:

A computer is another important tool that scientists use. Tell three ways that Mr. Perez could use it in his work with the bluebirds.

Use 1: **Possible answers: write reports, make charts and graphs, do research, and communicate with other scientists**

Use 2:

Use 3:

Week #2: The Metric System — Day #1

When people in the United States measure, they use the customary system. Length is measured in inches and feet. Weight is measured in pounds. Capacity uses cups, pints, and gallons. Most other people in the world use the metric system. Every measurement is based on a unit of ten. A meter measures length. There are 100 centimeters in a meter. A liter measures capacity. There are 100 centiliters in a liter. Scientists all over the world, even in the United States, use the metric system when they work.

Possible answer: Even if scientists cannot understand the words, they can understand all the measurements of the things in the world.

Day #2

Complete the chart with the correct metric units.

Length	Capacity	Weight
1.0 meter	1.0 liter	1.0 gram
10.0 decimeters	**10.0** deciliters	10.0 decigrams
100.0 centimeters	100.0 centiliters	100.0 centigrams
1000.0 millimeters	1000.0 milliliters	**1000.0** milligrams

Day #3

Write the abbreviation for each metric measurement word.

1. liter **L**
2. gram **g**
3. meter **m**
4. centimeter **cm**
5. milliliter **mL**
6. kilogram **kg**
7. millimeter **mm**
8. decigram **dg**
9. kilometer **km**

Day #4

In the metric system, temperature is measured in degrees Celsius (°C). Water freezes at 0°C and boils at 100°C. The temperature on a hot summer day would be around 30°C.

What is the temperature? Circle the best estimate.

1. a popsicle — **(0°C)** 45°C
2. a cup of hot chocolate — 15°C **(85°C)**
3. room temperature — **(20°C)** 60°F
4. swimming weather — 5°C **(35°C)**

Week #2: The Metric System — Assessment #2

Look at each metric measurement. Write the name of an object that is about that measurement.

For 1–6, answers will vary. Possible answers are given.

1. 8 centimeters — **a crayon**
2. 1 meter — **the height of a desk**
3. 1 liter — **a bottle of water**
4. 100 milliliters — **a can of soup**
5. 1 gram — **a paper clip**
6. 2 kilograms — **a bag of potatoes**

Use a metric ruler. Draw lines to show each length.

7. 30 millimeters
8. 48 millimeters
9. 12 centimeters
10. 7 centimeters

11. Write the temperature shown on the thermometer. Tell what you would do in this weather.

The temperature is 22°C. Accept reasonable answers that include activities for playing outside on a warm day.

Published by Frank Schaffer Publications. Copyright protected. 0-7682-3523-5 Science 4 Today

Answer Key

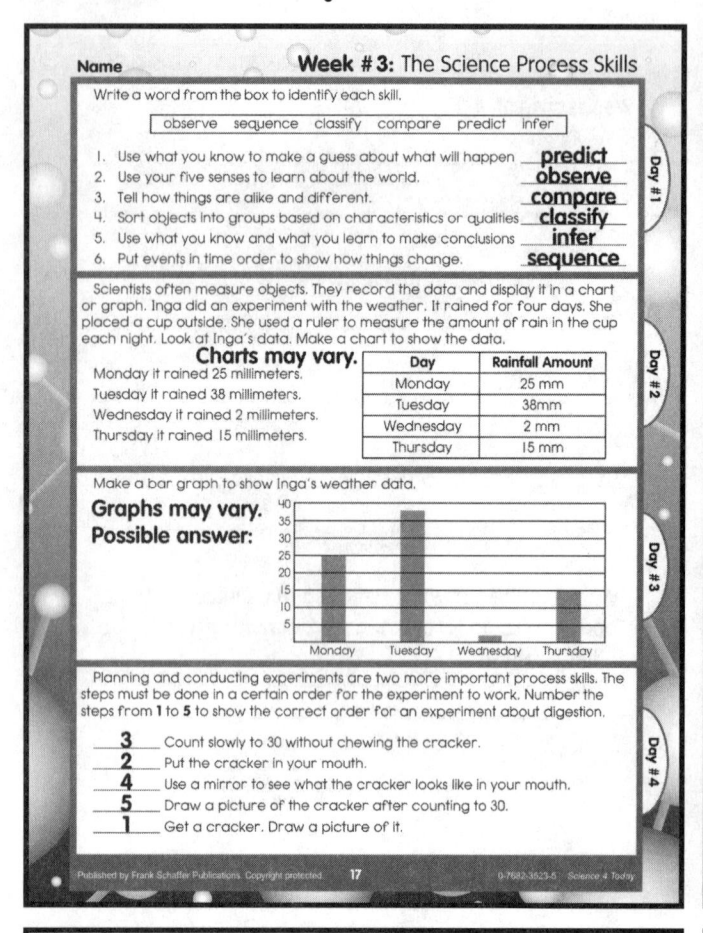

Week #3: The Science Process Skills

Write a word from the box to identify each skill.

observe   sequence   classify   compare   predict   infer

1. Use what you know to make a guess about what will happen. — **predict**
2. Use your five senses to learn about the world. — **observe**
3. Tell how things are alike and different. — **compare**
4. Sort objects into groups based on characteristics or qualities. — **classify**
5. Use what you know and what you learn to make conclusions. — **infer**
6. Put events in time order to show how things change. — **sequence**

Scientists often measure objects. They record the data and display it in a chart or graph. Inga did an experiment with the weather. It rained for four days. She placed a cup outside. She used a ruler to measure the amount of rain in the cup each night. Look at Inga's data. Make a chart to show the data.

Charts may vary.
Monday it rained 25 millimeters.
Tuesday it rained 38 millimeters.
Wednesday it rained 2 millimeters.
Thursday it rained 15 millimeters.

Day	Rainfall Amount
Monday	25 mm
Tuesday	38 mm
Wednesday	2 mm
Thursday	15 mm

Make a bar graph to show Inga's weather data.

Graphs may vary. Possible answer:

Planning and conducting experiments are two more important process skills. The steps must be done in a certain order for the experiment to work. Number the steps from 1 to 5 to show the correct order for an experiment about digestion.

- **3** Count slowly to 30 without chewing the cracker.
- **2** Put the cracker in your mouth.
- **4** Use a mirror to see what the cracker looks like in your mouth.
- **5** Draw a picture of the cracker after counting to 30.
- **1** Get a cracker. Draw a picture of it.

Week #3: The Science Process Skills

Assessment #3

Read the paragraph.

Manny got a good grade on his science test. He decided to put the test on the refrigerator to surprise his mom. He used a magnet to hold the paper on the refrigerator. Manny felt the pull of the magnet as it got close to the steel of the refrigerator. He wondered what else the magnet would stick to. So, he decided to find out. Manny got a dime, paper clip, straight pin, scissors, and aluminum foil. He thought that the dime, pin, and scissors would stick to the magnet, but the others would not. Next, he put the magnet next to each object and watched what happened. If the object stuck to the magnet, he put it in one group. If it didn't, he put the item in a different group. He drew a chart to show his results. Manny guessed that the foil and the dime did not have steel in them because they did not stick to the magnet.

Name at least four science process skills Manny used. Tell how he used the skills.

Manny planned and conducted an experiment to see what items would stick to a magnet.
He predicted which objects would stick to the magnet.
He observed what happened when the magnet got close to each item.
He classified the items as being magnetic or not.
He displayed the data in a chart.
Manny inferred that some items were not made of steel because they did not stick to the magnet.

Week #4: The Scientific Method

When scientists see a problem, they want to find an answer. They follow steps in a specific order. The steps are called the *scientific method*.

Why do scientists use the scientific method?
Possible answer: It is an organized way to make sure that a problem is solved fully and without mistakes.

What might happen if a scientist did not follow the steps of the scientific method in order?
Possible answer: Other scientists could not repeat the experiment and might not believe the results.

Write numbers 1 to 8 to show the order of the steps in the scientific method.

- **4** Observation
- **6** Comparison
- **1** Problem
- **5** Conclusion
- **8** Resources
- **2** Hypothesis
- **7** Presentation
- **3** Experimentation

Write the name of the step being described.

1. Plan and conduct an investigation or activity. — **experimentation**
2. Predict what the results of the investigation will be. — **hypothesis**
3. Prepare and share a report that shows the data. — **presentation**
4. Draw a conclusion from the results of the investigation. — **conclusion**

Fill in the circle next to the example that is a good hypothesis.

1. A. Which melts more quickly—ice cream or ice cubes?
   B. Butterflies are pretty.
   ● Animals can move seeds.
   D. Do worms make the soil better?

2. A. Maple trees are tall.
   ● Plants need sunlight to grow.
   C. How much does a cactus grow in one year?
   D. I think the rose is the best flower.

Week #4: The Scientific Method

Assessment #4

Think about an experiment that you did. Describe what you did and which steps of the scientific method you used.

Answers will vary.

0-7682-3523-5   *Science 4 Today*

Answer Key

Week #5: A Good Scientist

Scientists have important characteristics that help them do their best work. Check the characteristics that you think are important for a scientist to have.

- ✓ curious
- ✓ patient
- ✓ creative
- ✓ watchful
- ___ speedy
- ___ uninterested
- ___ careless
- ✓ eager
- ✓ persistent

Choose two characteristics. Tell why they are important qualities for a scientist to have.

Answers will vary.

Communication is another important characteristic of a good scientist. Why must a scientist have this quality?

Possible answer: Scientists must be able to share their findings so that people can learn more about the world. Other scientists use the info and build on it.

What are two ways that a scientist might communicate?

Most likely answers: They can write reports and speak at meetings.

Read the paragraph. Then, answer the question.

Alexander Graham Bell was a scientist. He became interested in sounds when he was a boy. He studied how people talked as he got older. Bell got an idea of a way to send sound through a wire. He asked Tom Watson, who knew about electricity, to help make a machine that could do this. The men worked on several devices for a year before finding one that worked. They invented the telephone in 1876.

What were two characteristics that made Bell a good scientist? Explain.

He was eager to learn about sound, and he was persistent.

Read the paragraph. Then, answer the question.

Jane Goodall liked chimpanzees. She went to Africa to learn about them. She spent many years living in a tent in the jungle to watch them. She took careful notes about what she saw. Goodall also photographed and filmed the animals in their natural habitats. She found out many new facts about the chimpanzees and the skills they had. Goodall wrote books and gave talks about her discoveries.

What were two characteristics that made Goodall a good scientist? Explain.

She was watchful, and she communicated information she learned.

Week #5: A Good Scientist — Assessment #5

Would you make a good scientist? Why or why not? Write a paragraph that explains at least three characteristics that prove your opinion.

Accept reasonable answers.

Week #6: Matter

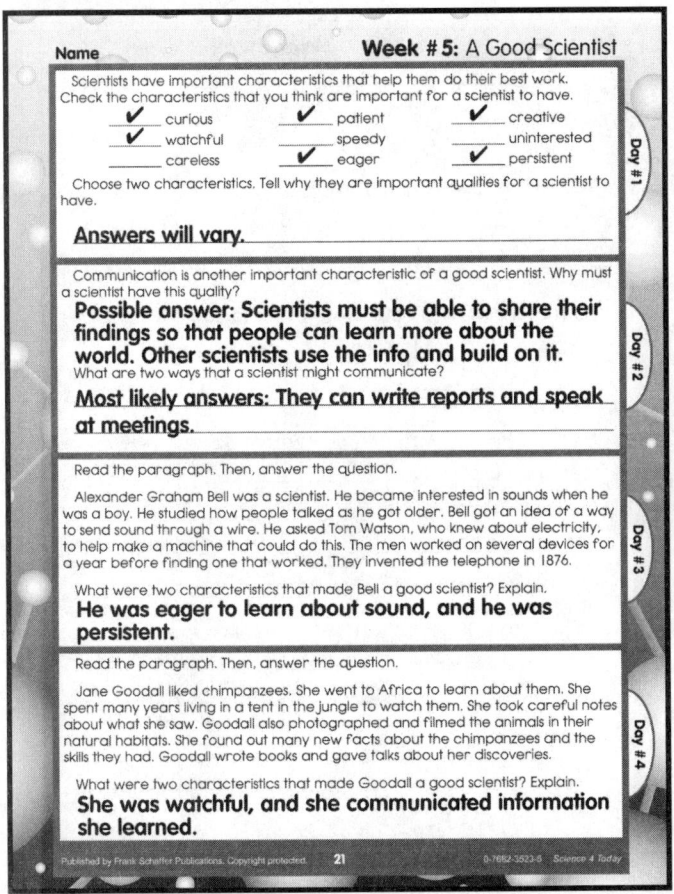

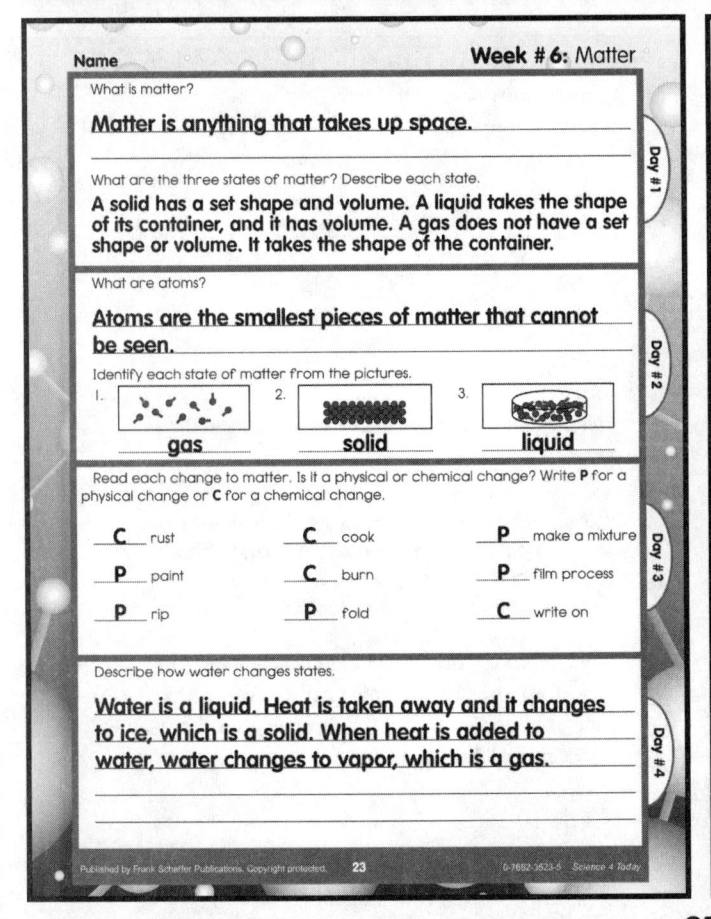

What is matter?

Matter is anything that takes up space.

What are the three states of matter? Describe each state.

A solid has a set shape and volume. A liquid takes the shape of its container, and it has volume. A gas does not have a set shape or volume. It takes the shape of the container.

What are atoms?

Atoms are the smallest pieces of matter that cannot be seen.

Identify each state of matter from the pictures.

1. gas
2. solid
3. liquid

Read each change to matter. Is it a physical or chemical change? Write P for a physical change or C for a chemical change.

- C rust
- C cook
- P make a mixture
- P paint
- C burn
- P film process
- P rip
- P fold
- C write on

Describe how water changes states.

Water is a liquid. Heat is taken away and it changes to ice, which is a solid. When heat is added to water, water changes to vapor, which is a gas.

Week #6: Matter — Assessment #6

Answer the questions.

1. Read each item. Write the name of its state.

   - desk **solid**
   - orange juice **liquid**
   - air **gas**
   - water vapor **gas**
   - book **solid**
   - hot chocolate **liquid**

2. Why does a chair never change shape?

   A chair is a solid. The atoms are packed tightly together, so they cannot move.

3. Imagine that you have two different objects that are the same size. Do these items always have the same mass? Explain.

   No. One object may have more matter in it, so it will be heavier.

4. Think about making cookies. Describe the physical and chemical changes that take place.

   When the flour, sugar, eggs, and other ingredients are mixed together, it is a physical change. When heat is added, and the cookies bake, it is a chemical change.

5. Why does a shovel rust if it is left outside in the rain?

   Air mixes with water to make a chemical change called rust.

Answer Key

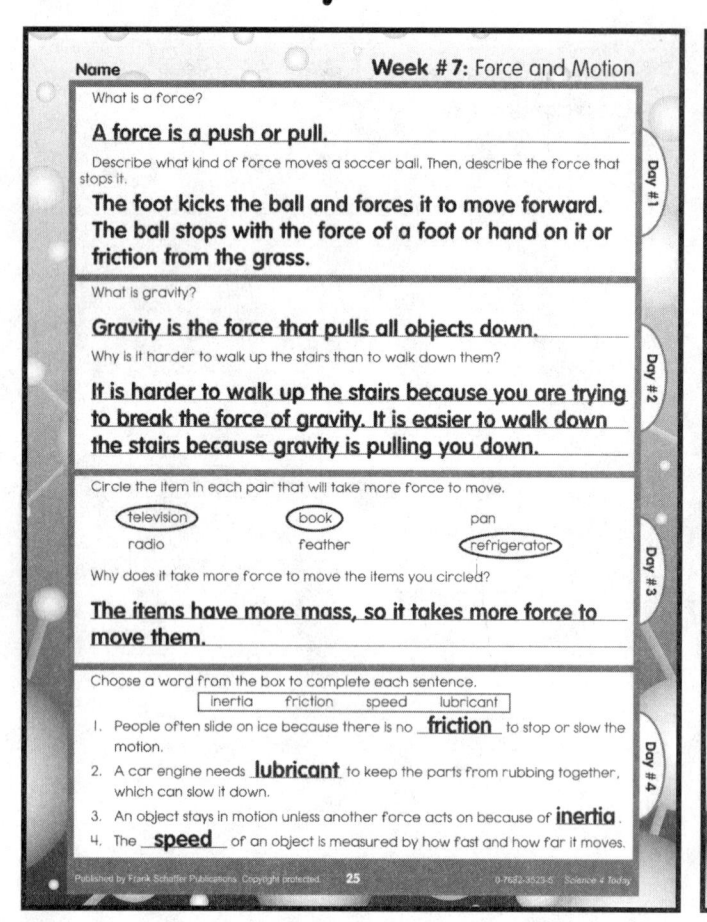

Week #7: Force and Motion

What is a force?
A force is a push or pull.

Describe what kind of force moves a soccer ball. Then, describe the force that stops it.
The foot kicks the ball and forces it to move forward. The ball stops with the force of a foot or hand on it or friction from the grass.

What is gravity?
Gravity is the force that pulls all objects down.

Why is it harder to walk up the stairs than to walk down them?
It is harder to walk up the stairs because you are trying to break the force of gravity. It is easier to walk down the stairs because gravity is pulling you down.

Circle the item in each pair that will take more force to move.
- (television) / radio
- (book) / feather
- pan / (refrigerator)

Why does it take more force to move the items you circled?
The items have more mass, so it takes more force to move them.

Choose a word from the box to complete each sentence.
inertia   friction   speed   lubricant

1. People often slide on ice because there is no **friction** to stop or slow the motion.
2. A car engine needs **lubricant** to keep the parts from rubbing together, which can slow it down.
3. An object stays in motion unless another force acts on because of **inertia**.
4. The **speed** of an object is measured by how fast and how far it moves.

Assessment #7

Answer the questions.

1. How do you know if a force is working?
You will see something move.

2. Imagine that you drop a tennis ball and a bag of potatoes at the same time. Explain what will happen and why.
Both objects will hit the ground at the same time because the pull of gravity is the same.

3. Would it be easier to ride your bike along a gravel or cement driveway? Explain.
It would be easier to ride on cement because there would be less friction.

Fill in the circle next to the best answer.

4. Two classes are having a tug-of-war. Mr. Jackson's class is pulling Ms. Otto's class closer toward the line. What is happening?
   - (A) Mr. Jackson's class is pulling with less force.
   - **(B) Mrs. Otto's class is pulling with less force.**
   - (C) Mrs. Otto's class is pulling with more force.
   - (D) Both teams are pulling with the same force.

5. Tia and Yukio are racing their bikes to the park. They leave at the exact same time and follow the same path, but Yukio gets to the park first. Why did Yukio get there first?
   - (A) Tia had less inertia.
   - **(C) Yukio had more speed.**
   - (B) Tia had more friction.
   - (D) Gravity pulled Yukio.

Week #8: Machines

What is work?
Work is using a force to move an object over a distance.

Vince used 3 newtons to move a box 3 meters. Mark used 4 newtons to move the box 2 meters. Who did more work? Explain.
Vince did more work because he did 9 newton-meters and Mark only did 8 newton-meters.

What kind of simple machine is each object? Write the name of the machine.
1. seesaw — lever
2. slide — inclined plane
3. fork — wedge
4. flag pole — pulley
5. screw — screw
6. fishing rod reel — wheel and axel

What is a compound machine?
A compound machine is a machine that has two or more simple machines that work together to make work even easier.

Name the simple machines in a pair of scissors.
Each blade is a wedge. The handles are levers. Where the handles meet is the fulcrum.

Beth is opening a can of paint using a screwdriver. Explain two ways that Beth can use the screwdriver to make different simple machines.
Beth can use the screwdriver as a wheel and axel by putting the tip of the tool into the opening and twisting her wrist to lift the lid. She can also use the screwdriver as a lever to pry the lid straight up.

Assessment #8

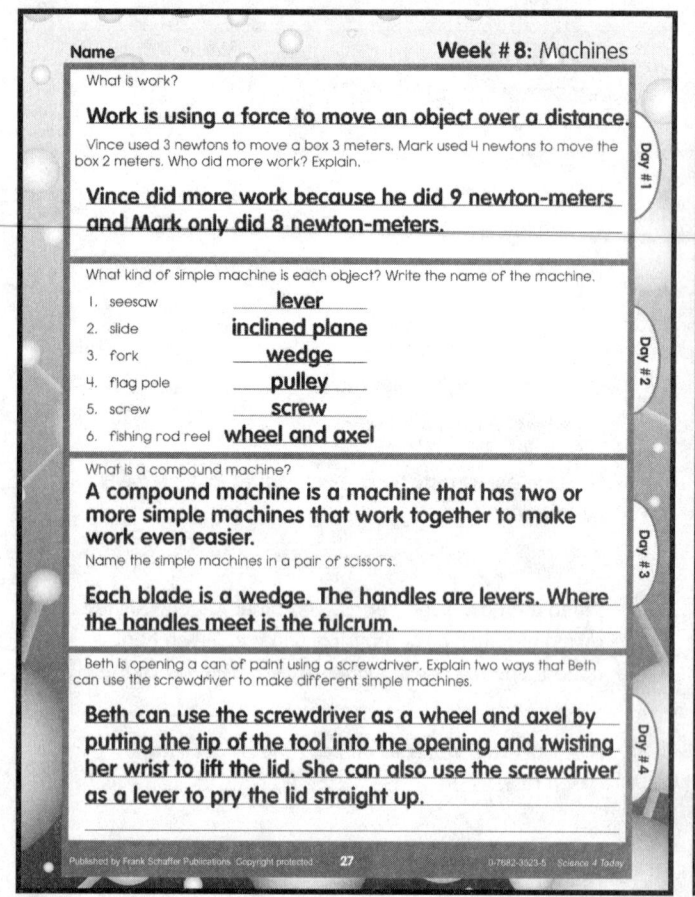

Fill in the circle next to the best answer.

1. What simple machine is made when a flat surface is set at an angle to another surface?
   - (A) a screw
   - (C) pulley
   - **(B) an inclined plane**
   - (D) wheel and axle

2. Which tool is not an example of a lever?
   - (A) tweezers
   - (C) hammer
   - (B) nut cracker
   - **(D) rake**

Answer the questions.

3. Shina is pushing on a door, but it does not open. Is she doing work? Explain.
Shina did not do work because the door did not move.

4. How do simple machines make work easier?
You do not have to use as much force with most simple machines. Simple machines also change the direction of the force. Some can do both.

5. Which simple machines are in a wheelbarrow? Tell how each makes work easier.
A wheelbarrow has a wheel and axle that helps roll a load with less force. It also has a lever, which changes the direction of the force so that a heavy load can be lifted more easily.

Answer Key

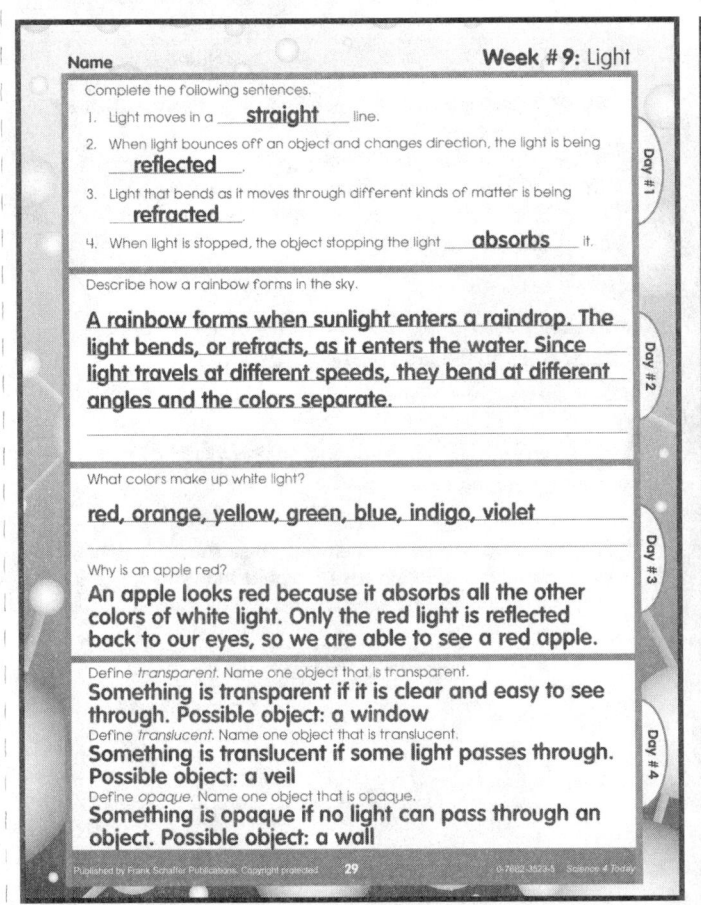

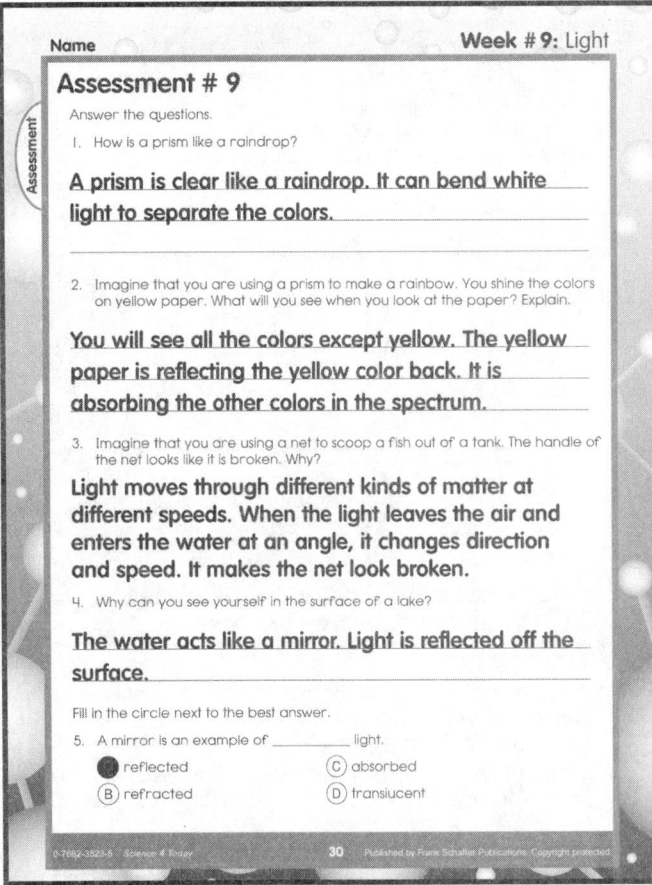

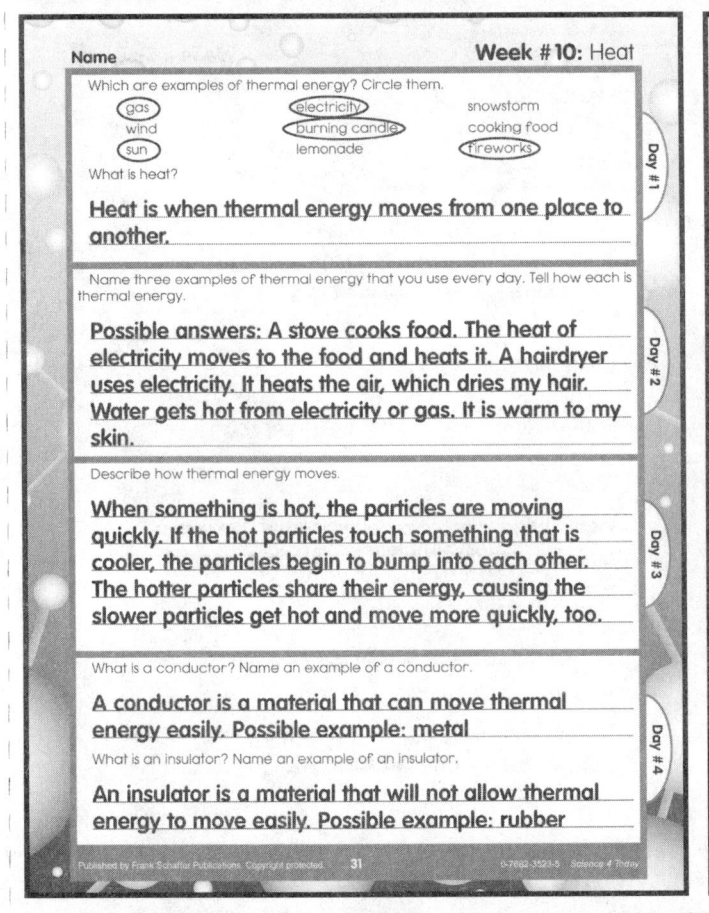

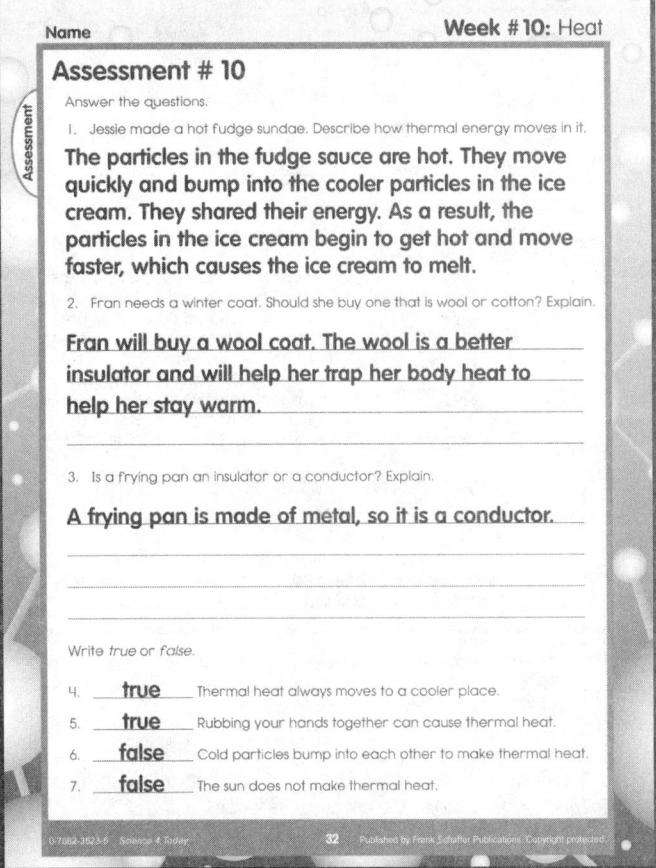

Week #9: Light

Complete the following sentences.

1. Light moves in a **straight** line.
2. When light bounces off an object and changes direction, the light is being **reflected**.
3. Light that bends as it moves through different kinds of matter is being **refracted**.
4. When light is stopped, the object stopping the light **absorbs** it.

Describe how a rainbow forms in the sky.

A rainbow forms when sunlight enters a raindrop. The light bends, or refracts, as it enters the water. Since light travels at different speeds, they bend at different angles and the colors separate.

What colors make up white light?

red, orange, yellow, green, blue, indigo, violet

Why is an apple red?

An apple looks red because it absorbs all the other colors of white light. Only the red light is reflected back to our eyes, so we are able to see a red apple.

Define transparent. Name one object that is transparent.
Something is transparent if it is clear and easy to see through. Possible object: a window

Define translucent. Name one object that is translucent.
Something is translucent if some light passes through. Possible object: a veil

Define opaque. Name one object that is opaque.
Something is opaque if no light can pass through an object. Possible object: a wall

Assessment #9 — Week #9: Light

Answer the questions.

1. How is a prism like a raindrop?

A prism is clear like a raindrop. It can bend white light to separate the colors.

2. Imagine that you are using a prism to make a rainbow. You shine the colors on yellow paper. What will you see when you look at the paper? Explain.

You will see all the colors except yellow. The yellow paper is reflecting the yellow color back. It is absorbing the other colors in the spectrum.

3. Imagine that you are using a net to scoop a fish out of a tank. The handle of the net looks like it is broken. Why?

Light moves through different kinds of matter at different speeds. When the light leaves the air and enters the water at an angle, it changes direction and speed. It makes the net look broken.

4. Why can you see yourself in the surface of a lake?

The water acts like a mirror. Light is reflected off the surface.

Fill in the circle next to the best answer.

5. A mirror is an example of _____ light.
   - ● A reflected
   - ○ B refracted
   - ○ C absorbed
   - ○ D translucent

Week #10: Heat

Which are examples of thermal energy? Circle them.

(gas), (electricity), snowstorm, wind, (burning candle), cooking food, (sun), lemonade, (fireworks)

What is heat?

Heat is when thermal energy moves from one place to another.

Name three examples of thermal energy that you use every day. Tell how each is thermal energy.

Possible answers: A stove cooks food. The heat of electricity moves to the food and heats it. A hairdryer uses electricity. It heats the air, which dries my hair. Water gets hot from electricity or gas. It is warm to my skin.

Describe how thermal energy moves.

When something is hot, the particles are moving quickly. If the hot particles touch something that is cooler, the particles begin to bump into each other. The hotter particles share their energy, causing the slower particles get hot and move more quickly, too.

What is a conductor? Name an example of a conductor.

A conductor is a material that can move thermal energy easily. Possible example: metal

What is an insulator? Name an example of an insulator.

An insulator is a material that will not allow thermal energy to move easily. Possible example: rubber

Assessment #10 — Week #10: Heat

Answer the questions.

1. Jessie made a hot fudge sundae. Describe how thermal energy moves in it.

The particles in the fudge sauce are hot. They move quickly and bump into the cooler particles in the ice cream. They shared their energy. As a result, the particles in the ice cream begin to get hot and move faster, which causes the ice cream to melt.

2. Fran needs a winter coat. Should she buy one that is wool or cotton? Explain.

Fran will buy a wool coat. The wool is a better insulator and will help her trap her body heat to help her stay warm.

3. Is a frying pan an insulator or a conductor? Explain.

A frying pan is made of metal, so it is a conductor.

Write true or false.

4. **true** Thermal heat always moves to a cooler place.
5. **true** Rubbing your hands together can cause thermal heat.
6. **false** Cold particles bump into each other to make thermal heat.
7. **false** The sun does not make thermal heat.

Answer Key

Week #11: Electricity — Day #1

What four kinds of energy can electricity make? Write the name of a device that is an example of each.

1. **Possible answers: light, lamp**
2. **sound, door bell**
3. **heat, oven**
4. **movement, fan**

What are the three parts of an atom?

electron, proton, neutron

An electron has a **negative** charge.
A proton has a **positive** charge.
A neutron has a **neutral** charge.

Label the diagram to show the parts of a circuit.

energy source, wire, end source, switch

Will the light bulb in the diagram above light? Explain.

The bulb will light because the circuit is a closed circuit, which means that all parts are connected.

Write three electric safety rules.

Possible answers: Do not go near electric power lines that are on the ground. Keep electric appliances away from water. Don't fly kites near power lines. Don't stick things into outlets. Unplug appliances that are not often used. Keep electric cords away from babies and pets. Cover outlets that are not in use.

Week #11: Electricity — Assessment #11

Answer the questions.

1. Why is your body a good conductor of electricity?

The body is made mostly of water. Water is a good conductor of electricity, so an electric current can flow easily in the body.

2. Why do workers who repair electric power lines wear rubber gloves instead of glass gloves?

Rubber gloves are an insulator and keep a current from entering the workers body.

3. If you turn on a light switch and the bulb does not glow, what might you guess about the circuit? Explain.

One part of the circuit is open and an electric current cannot flow through it.

4. Explain why you should stay inside during a lightning storm.

Lightning is a source of electricity. Since the body is a good conductor and stands up higher than many things, lighting can be attracted to it.

Darken the circle next to the best answer.

Which of the following is a source in a circuit?
- ● A a battery
- ○ C a switch
- ○ B a light bulb
- ○ D a wire

How does matter move in electricity?
- ○ A in a circle
- ○ C in opposite directions
- ○ B up and down
- ● in the same direction

Week #12: Plants — Day #1

What four things do plants need?

Plants need water, air, sunlight, and soil.

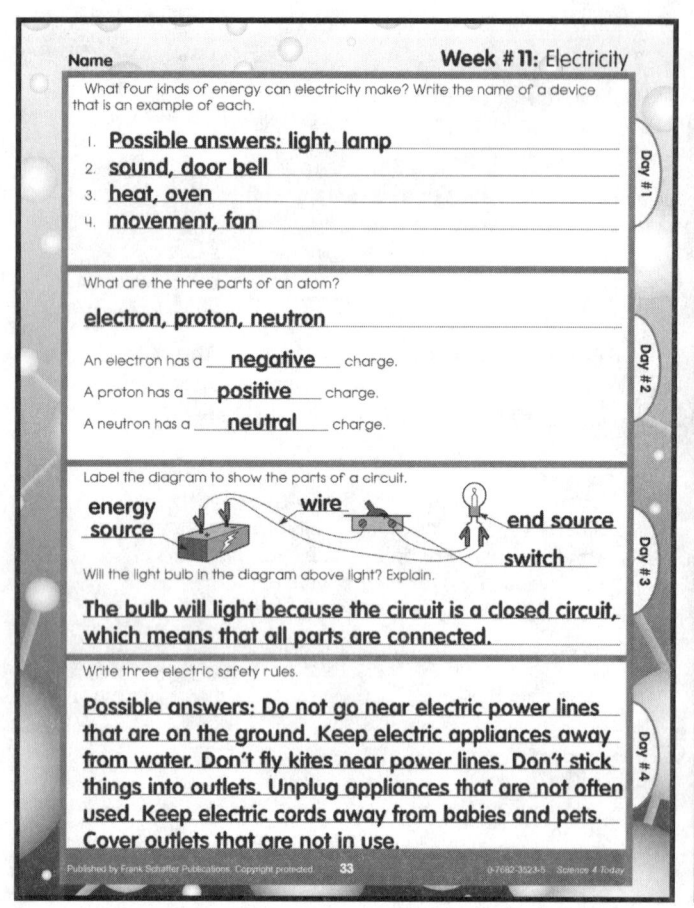

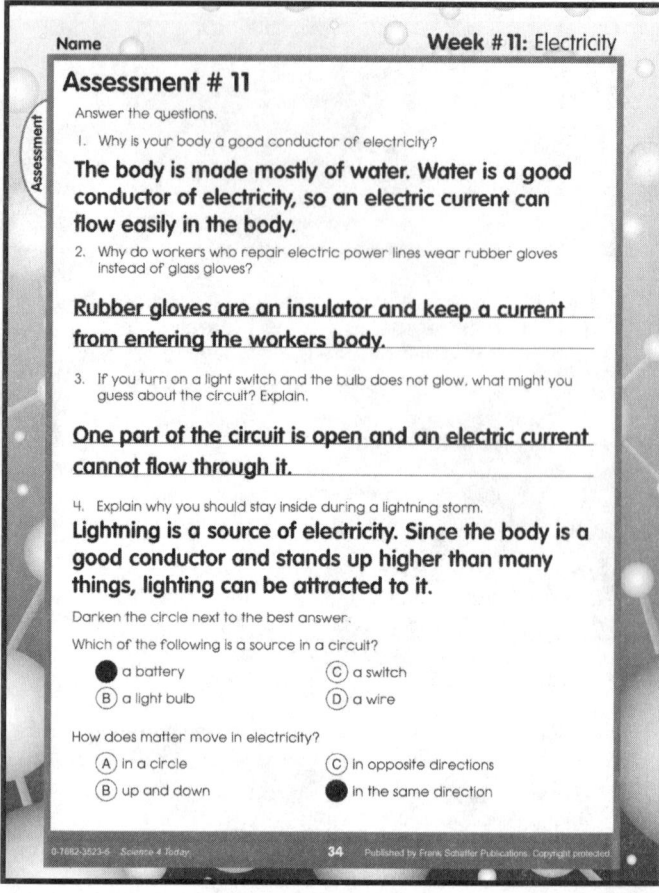

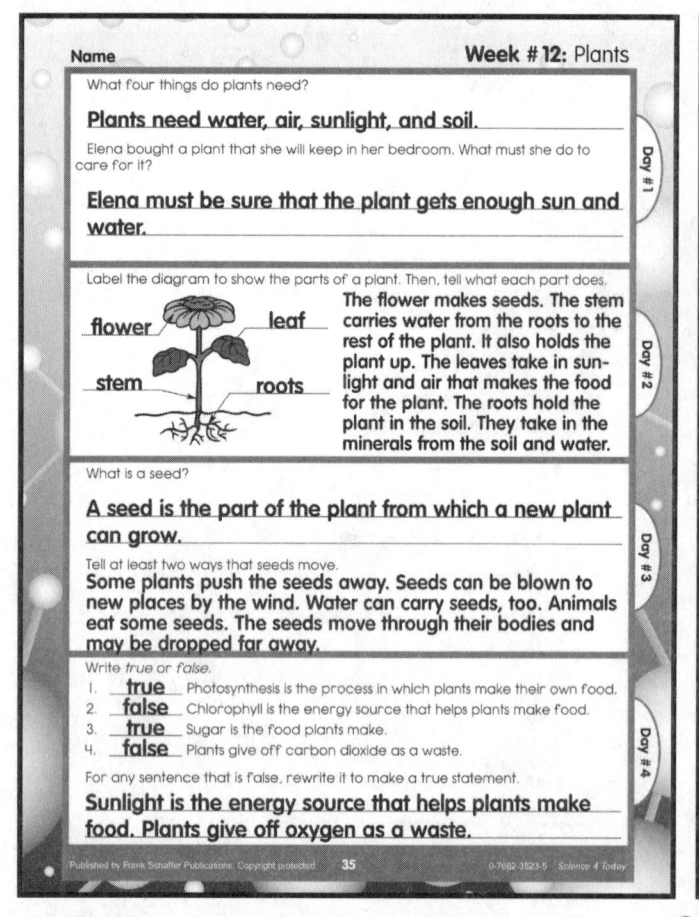

Elena bought a plant that she will keep in her bedroom. What must she do to care for it?

Elena must be sure that the plant gets enough sun and water.

Label the diagram to show the parts of a plant. Then, tell what each part does.

flower, leaf, stem, roots

The flower makes seeds. The stem carries water from the roots to the rest of the plant. It also holds the plant up. The leaves take in sunlight and air that makes the food for the plant. The roots hold the plant in the soil. They take in the minerals from the soil and water.

What is a seed?

A seed is the part of the plant from which a new plant can grow.

Tell at least two ways that seeds move.

Some plants push the seeds away. Seeds can be blown to new places by the wind. Water can carry seeds, too. Animals eat some seeds. The seeds move through their bodies and may be dropped far away.

Write *true* or *false*.
1. **true** Photosynthesis is the process in which plants make their own food.
2. **false** Chlorophyll is the energy source that helps plants make food.
3. **true** Sugar is the food plants make.
4. **false** Plants give off carbon dioxide as a waste.

For any sentence that is false, rewrite it to make a true statement.

Sunlight is the energy source that helps plants make food. Plants give off oxygen as a waste.

Week #12: Plants — Assessment #12

Answer the questions.

Asa does an experiment. She cuts a one-inch circle out of construction paper and paper clips it to the top of a leaf. After one week, she removes the paper circle. What will she see? Explain what has happened.

Asa will see an area the same size of the circle that is yellow or less green than the rest of the leaf. That part of the leaf was not able to get sunlight.

What do plants need to make food? What is this process called?

Plants need light, chlorophyll, carbon dioxide, and water to make food. The process is called photosynthesis.

Describe three ways that plants are important to people.

Possible answers:
They provide oxygen, food, shade, lumber to build with, and shelter for animals.

0-7682-3523-5 *Science 4 Today* — Published by Frank Schaffer Publications. Copyright protected.

Answer Key

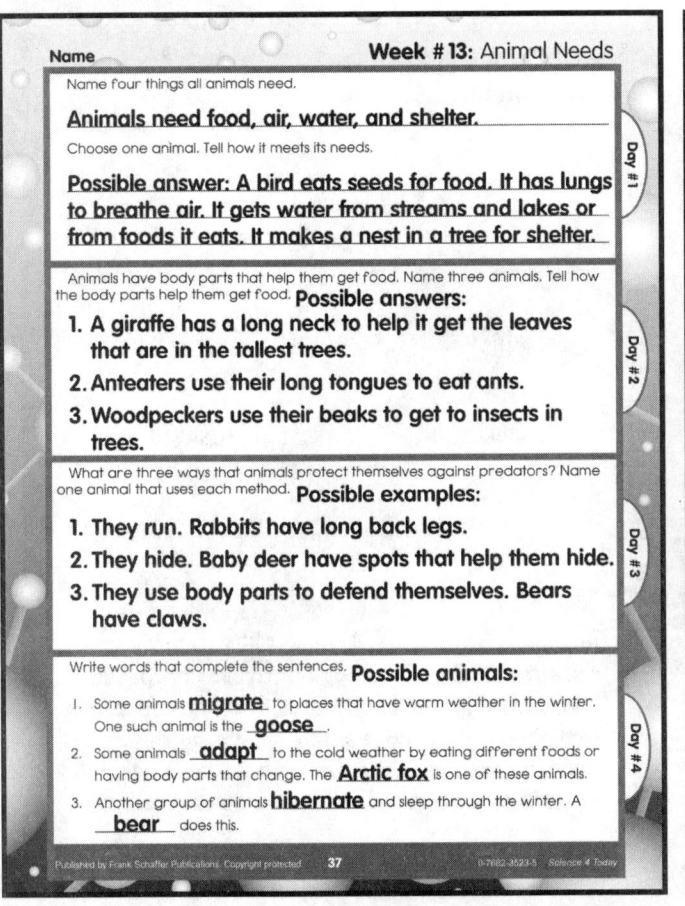

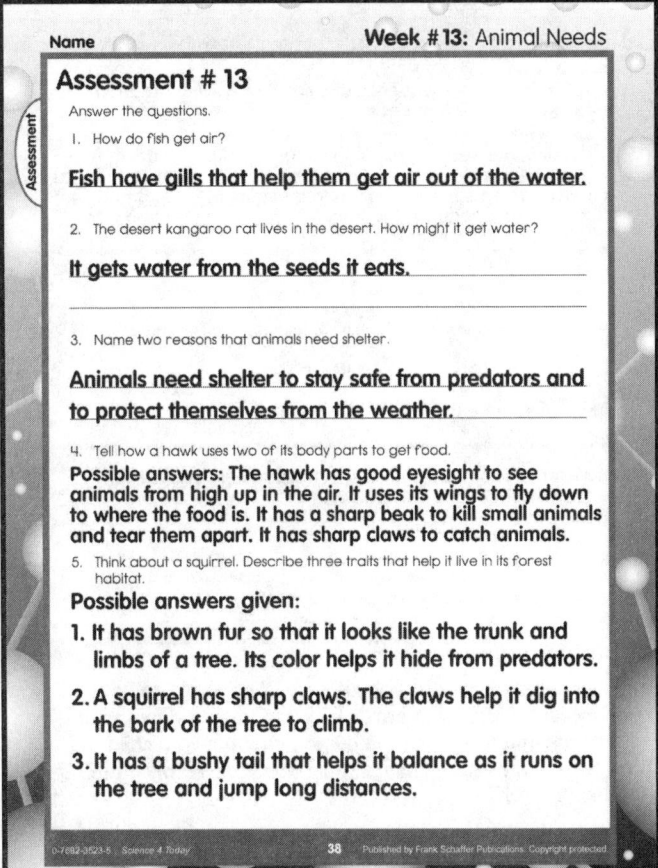

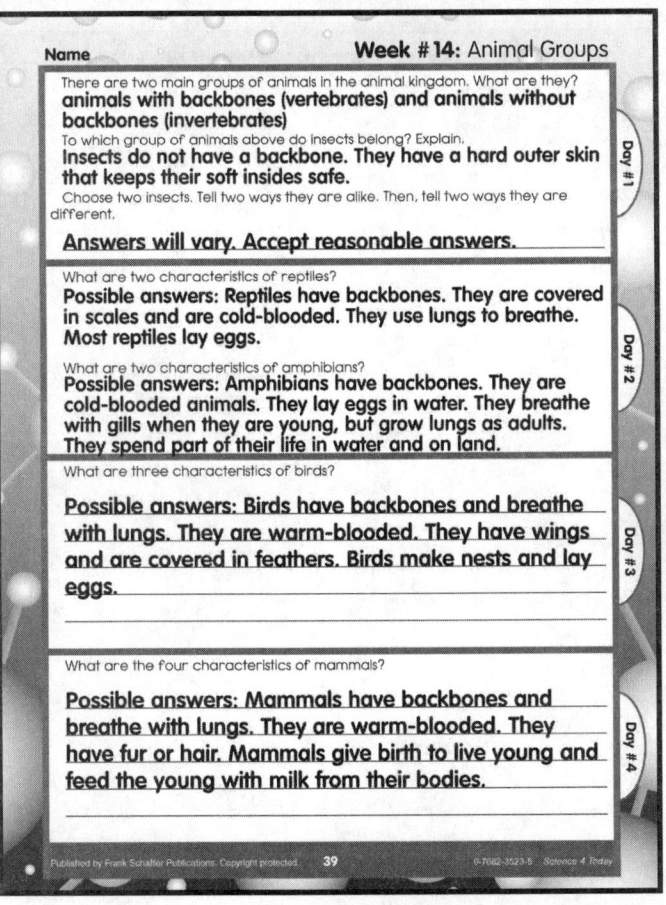

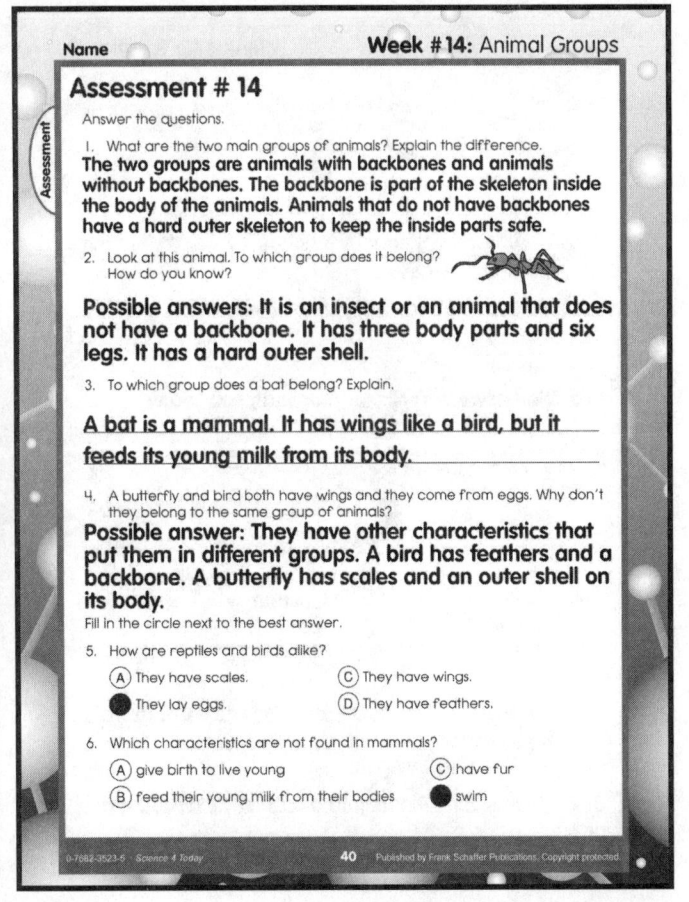

Week #13: Animal Needs

Name four things all animals need.
Animals need food, air, water, and shelter.

Choose one animal. Tell how it meets its needs.
Possible answer: A bird eats seeds for food. It has lungs to breathe air. It gets water from streams and lakes or from foods it eats. It makes a nest in a tree for shelter.

Animals have body parts that help them get food. Name three animals. Tell how the body parts help them get food. Possible answers:
1. A giraffe has a long neck to help it get the leaves that are in the tallest trees.
2. Anteaters use their long tongues to eat ants.
3. Woodpeckers use their beaks to get to insects in trees.

What are three ways that animals protect themselves against predators? Name one animal that uses each method. Possible examples:
1. They run. Rabbits have long back legs.
2. They hide. Baby deer have spots that help them hide.
3. They use body parts to defend themselves. Bears have claws.

Write words that complete the sentences. Possible animals:
1. Some animals **migrate** to places that have warm weather in the winter. One such animal is the **goose**.
2. Some animals **adapt** to the cold weather by eating different foods or having body parts that change. The **Arctic fox** is one of these animals.
3. Another group of animals **hibernate** and sleep through the winter. A **bear** does this.

Week #13: Animal Needs — Assessment #13

Answer the questions.

1. How do fish get air?
Fish have gills that help them get air out of the water.

2. The desert kangaroo rat lives in the desert. How might it get water?
It gets water from the seeds it eats.

3. Name two reasons that animals need shelter.
Animals need shelter to stay safe from predators and to protect themselves from the weather.

4. Tell how a hawk uses two of its body parts to get food.
Possible answers: The hawk has good eyesight to see animals from high up in the air. It uses its wings to fly down to where the food is. It has a sharp beak to kill small animals and tear them apart. It has sharp claws to catch animals.

5. Think about a squirrel. Describe three traits that help it live in its forest habitat.
Possible answers given:
1. It has brown fur so that it looks like the trunk and limbs of a tree. Its color helps it hide from predators.
2. A squirrel has sharp claws. The claws help it dig into the bark of the tree to climb.
3. It has a bushy tail that helps it balance as it runs on the tree and jump long distances.

Week #14: Animal Groups

There are two main groups of animals in the animal kingdom. What are they?
animals with backbones (vertebrates) and animals without backbones (invertebrates)

To which group of animals above do insects belong? Explain.
Insects do not have a backbone. They have a hard outer skin that keeps their soft insides safe.

Choose two insects. Tell two ways they are alike. Then, tell two ways they are different.
Answers will vary. Accept reasonable answers.

What are two characteristics of reptiles?
Possible answers: Reptiles have backbones. They are covered in scales and are cold-blooded. They use lungs to breathe. Most reptiles lay eggs.

What are two characteristics of amphibians?
Possible answers: Amphibians have backbones. They are cold-blooded animals. They lay eggs in water. They breathe with gills when they are young, but grow lungs as adults. They spend part of their life in water and on land.

What are three characteristics of birds?
Possible answers: Birds have backbones and breathe with lungs. They are warm-blooded. They have wings and are covered in feathers. Birds make nests and lay eggs.

What are the four characteristics of mammals?
Possible answers: Mammals have backbones and breathe with lungs. They are warm-blooded. They have fur or hair. Mammals give birth to live young and feed the young with milk from their bodies.

Week #14: Animal Groups — Assessment #14

Answer the questions.

1. What are the two main groups of animals? Explain the difference.
The two groups are animals with backbones and animals without backbones. The backbone is part of the skeleton inside the body of the animals. Animals that do not have backbones have a hard outer skeleton to keep the inside parts safe.

2. Look at this animal. To which group does it belong? How do you know?
Possible answers: It is an insect or an animal that does not have a backbone. It has three body parts and six legs. It has a hard outer shell.

3. To which group does a bat belong? Explain.
A bat is a mammal. It has wings like a bird, but it feeds its young milk from its body.

4. A butterfly and bird both have wings and they come from eggs. Why don't they belong to the same group of animals?
Possible answer: They have other characteristics that put them in different groups. A bird has feathers and a backbone. A butterfly has scales and an outer shell on its body.

Fill in the circle next to the best answer.

5. How are reptiles and birds alike?
A. They have scales.
C. They have wings.
● **They lay eggs.**
D. They have feathers.

6. Which characteristics are not found in mammals?
A. give birth to live young
C. have fur
B. feed their young milk from their bodies
● **swim**

Published by Frank Schaffer Publications. Copyright protected. 99 0-7682-3523-5 Science 4 Today

Answer Key

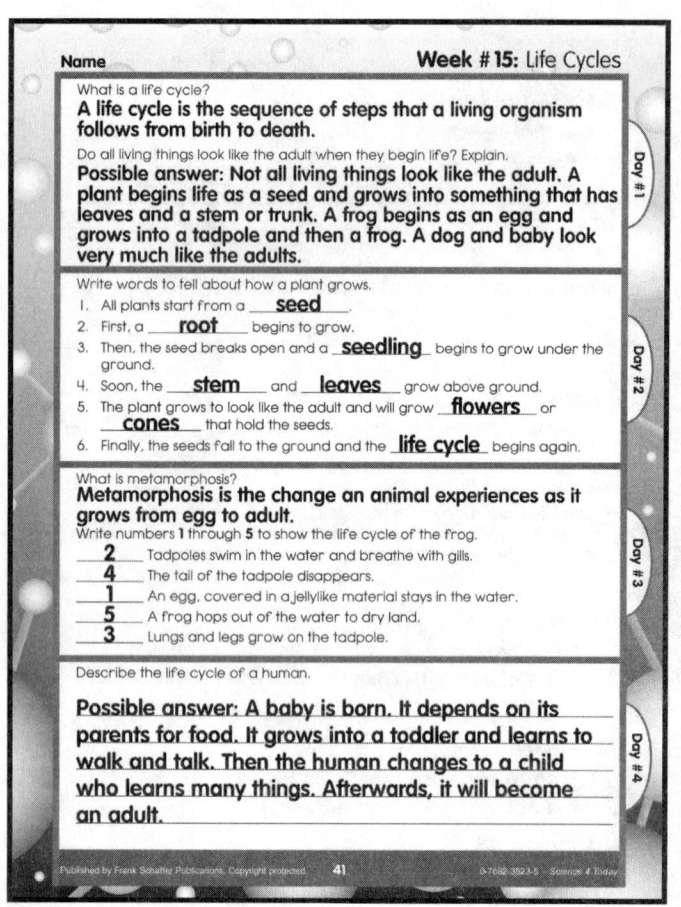

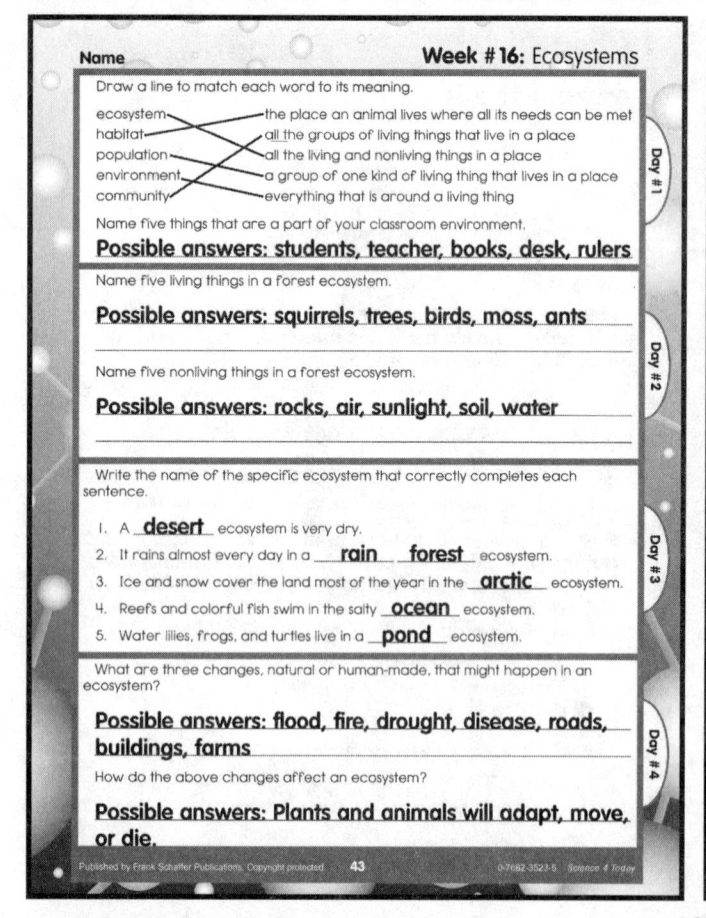

Week #15: Life Cycles

What is a life cycle?
A life cycle is the sequence of steps that a living organism follows from birth to death.

Do all living things look like the adult when they begin life? Explain.
Possible answer: Not all living things look like the adult. A plant begins life as a seed and grows into something that has leaves and a stem or trunk. A frog begins as an egg and grows into a tadpole and then a frog. A dog and baby look very much like the adults.

Write words to tell about how a plant grows.
1. All plants start from a **seed**.
2. First, a **root** begins to grow.
3. Then, the seed breaks open and a **seedling** begins to grow under the ground.
4. Soon, the **stem** and **leaves** grow above ground.
5. The plant grows to look like the adult and will grow **flowers** or **cones** that hold the seeds.
6. Finally, the seeds fall to the ground and the **life cycle** begins again.

What is metamorphosis?
Metamorphosis is the change an animal experiences as it grows from egg to adult.

Write numbers 1 through 5 to show the life cycle of the frog.
- **2** Tadpoles swim in the water and breathe with gills.
- **4** The tail of the tadpole disappears.
- **1** An egg, covered in a jellylike material stays in the water.
- **5** A frog hops out of the water to dry land.
- **3** Lungs and legs grow on the tadpole.

Describe the life cycle of a human.
Possible answer: A baby is born. It depends on its parents for food. It grows into a toddler and learns to walk and talk. Then the human changes to a child who learns many things. Afterwards, it will become an adult.

Assessment #15

Label the diagram to show the life cycle of a butterfly. Then, describe the cycle.

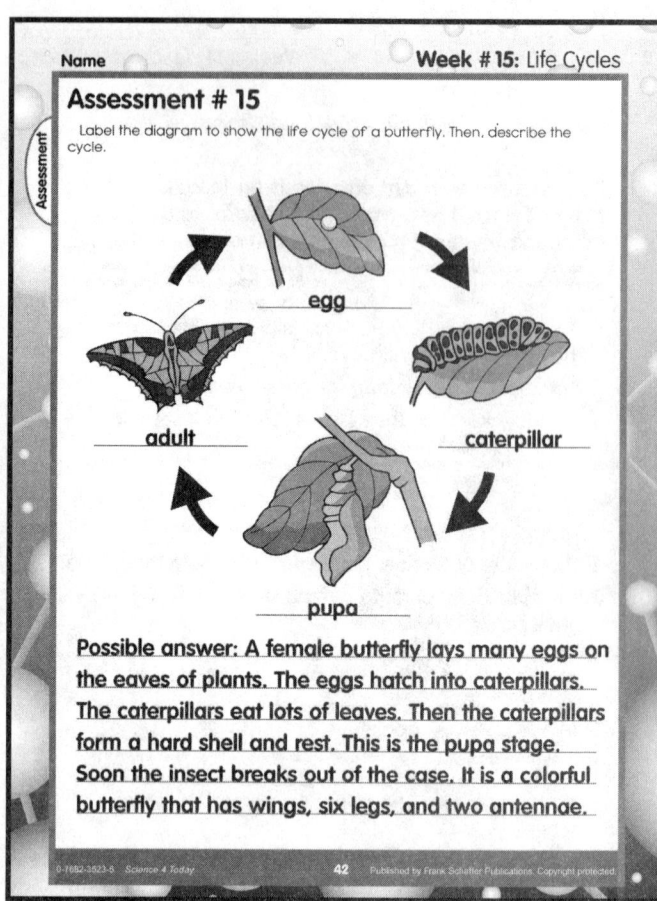

egg — caterpillar — pupa — adult

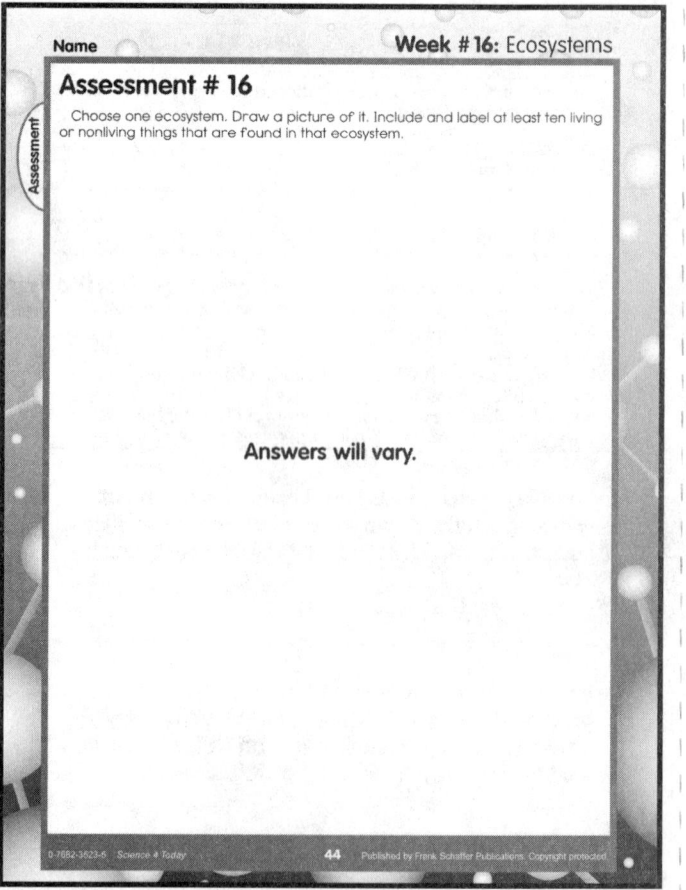

Possible answer: A female butterfly lays many eggs on the eaves of plants. The eggs hatch into caterpillars. The caterpillars eat lots of leaves. Then the caterpillars form a hard shell and rest. This is the pupa stage. Soon the insect breaks out of the case. It is a colorful butterfly that has wings, six legs, and two antennae.

Week #16: Ecosystems

Draw a line to match each word to its meaning.
- ecosystem — all the living and nonliving things that live in a place
- habitat — the place an animal lives where all its needs can be met
- population — a group of one kind of living thing that lives in a place
- environment — everything that is around a living thing
- community — all the groups of living things that live in a place

Name five things that are a part of your classroom environment.
Possible answers: students, teacher, books, desk, rulers

Name five living things in a forest ecosystem.
Possible answers: squirrels, trees, birds, moss, ants

Name five nonliving things in a forest ecosystem.
Possible answers: rocks, air, sunlight, soil, water

Write the name of the specific ecosystem that correctly completes each sentence.
1. A **desert** ecosystem is very dry.
2. It rains almost every day in a **rain forest** ecosystem.
3. Ice and snow cover the land most of the year in the **arctic** ecosystem.
4. Reefs and colorful fish swim in the salty **ocean** ecosystem.
5. Water lilies, frogs, and turtles live in a **pond** ecosystem.

What are three changes, natural or human-made, that might happen in an ecosystem?
Possible answers: flood, fire, drought, disease, roads, buildings, farms

How do the above changes affect an ecosystem?
Possible answers: Plants and animals will adapt, move, or die.

Assessment #16

Choose one ecosystem. Draw a picture of it. Include and label at least ten living or nonliving things that are found in that ecosystem.

Answers will vary.

Answer Key

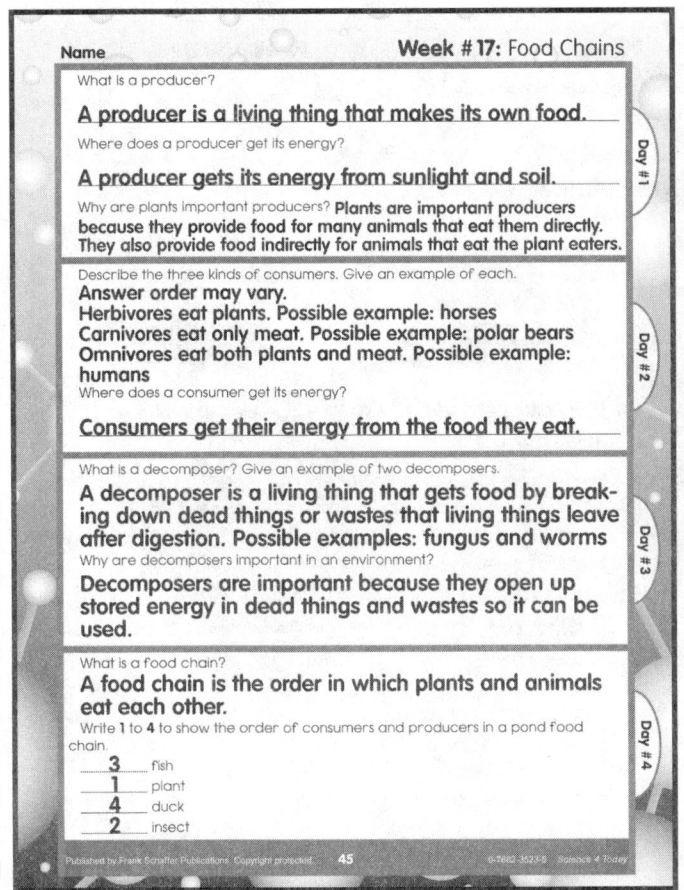

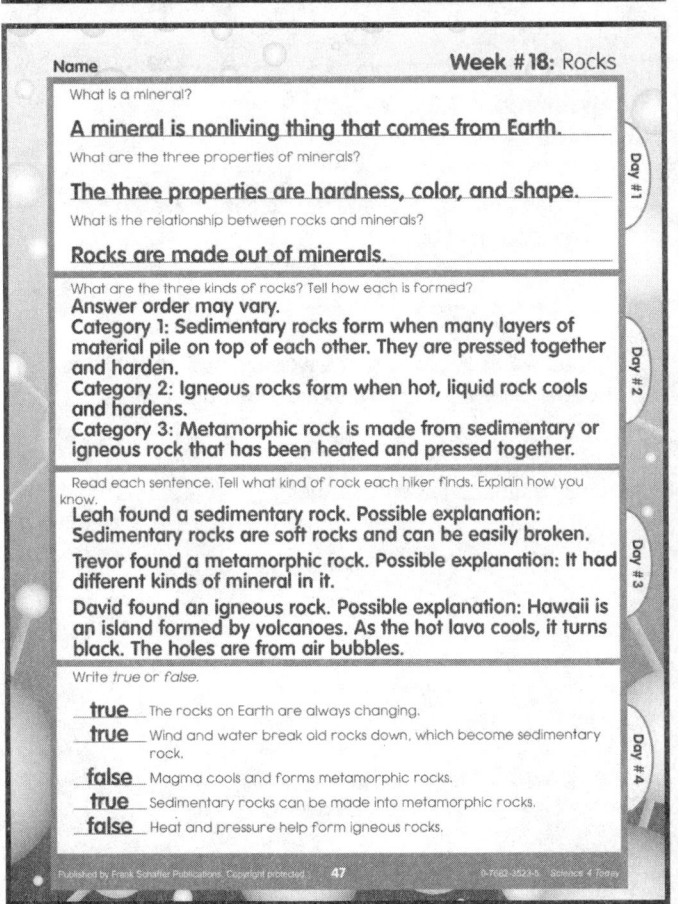

Week #17: Food Chains — Day #1–#4

What is a producer?
A producer is a living thing that makes its own food.

Where does a producer get its energy?
A producer gets its energy from sunlight and soil.

Why are plants important producers? Plants are important producers because they provide food for many animals that eat them directly. They also provide food indirectly for animals that eat the plant eaters.

Describe the three kinds of consumers. Give an example of each.
Answer order may vary.
Herbivores eat plants. Possible example: horses
Carnivores eat only meat. Possible example: polar bears
Omnivores eat both plants and meat. Possible example: humans

Where does a consumer get its energy?
Consumers get their energy from the food they eat.

What is a decomposer? Give an example of two decomposers.
A decomposer is a living thing that gets food by breaking down dead things or wastes that living things leave after digestion. Possible examples: fungus and worms

Why are decomposers important in an environment?
Decomposers are important because they open up stored energy in dead things and wastes so it can be used.

What is a food chain?
A food chain is the order in which plants and animals eat each other.

Write 1 to 4 to show the order of consumers and producers in a pond food chain.
- 3 fish
- 1 plant
- 4 duck
- 2 insect

Week #17: Food Chains — Assessment #17

1. Write P if the organism is a producer. Write C if the organism is a consumer. Write D if the organism is a decomposer.
   - C insect
   - P lettuce
   - C human
   - P rose
   - D mushroom
   - P tree
   - D worm
   - C bear
   - D bacteria

2. Describe the food chain below. Use the words in the box in your description. (consumer, producer, energy)

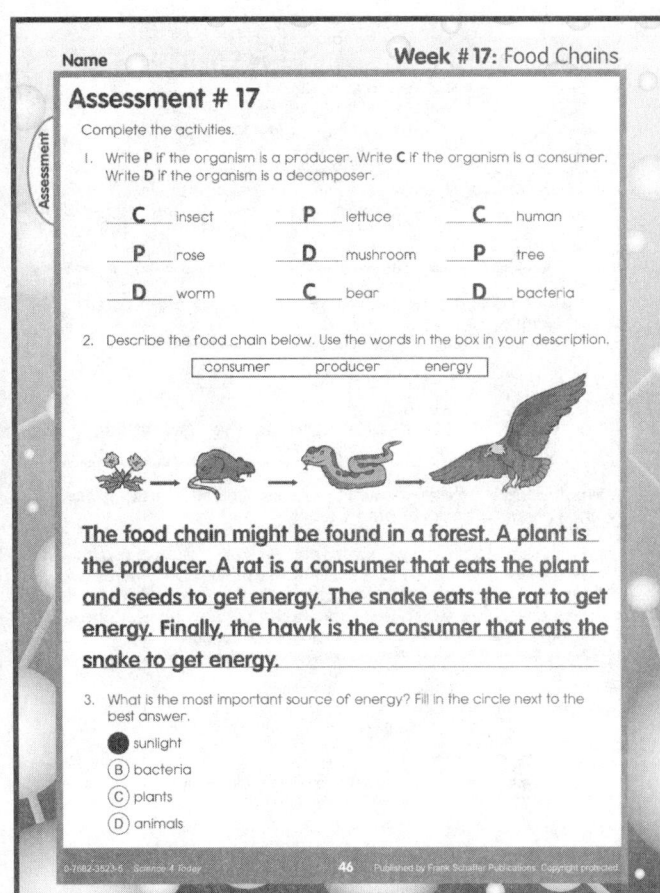

The food chain might be found in a forest. A plant is the producer. A rat is a consumer that eats the plant and seeds to get energy. The snake eats the rat to get energy. Finally, the hawk is the consumer that eats the snake to get energy.

3. What is the most important source of energy?
   - ● sunlight
   - ○ bacteria
   - ○ plants
   - ○ animals

Week #18: Rocks — Day #1–#4

What is a mineral?
A mineral is nonliving thing that comes from Earth.

What are the three properties of minerals?
The three properties are hardness, color, and shape.

What is the relationship between rocks and minerals?
Rocks are made out of minerals.

What are the three kinds of rocks? Tell how each is formed?
Answer order may vary.
Category 1: Sedimentary rocks form when many layers of material pile on top of each other. They are pressed together and harden.
Category 2: Igneous rocks form when hot, liquid rock cools and hardens.
Category 3: Metamorphic rock is made from sedimentary or igneous rock that has been heated and pressed together.

Read each sentence. Tell what kind of rock each hiker finds. Explain how you know.
Leah found a sedimentary rock. Possible explanation: Sedimentary rocks are soft rocks and can be easily broken.
Trevor found a metamorphic rock. Possible explanation: It had different kinds of mineral in it.
David found an igneous rock. Possible explanation: Hawaii is an island formed by volcanoes. As the hot lava cools, it turns black. The holes are from air bubbles.

Write true or false.
- true The rocks on Earth are always changing.
- true Wind and water break old rocks down, which become sedimentary rock.
- false Magma cools and forms metamorphic rocks.
- true Sedimentary rocks can be made into metamorphic rocks.
- false Heat and pressure help form igneous rocks.

Week #18: Rocks — Assessment #18

1. How do rocks form and change? Write the names of the kinds of rocks to complete the rock cycle.

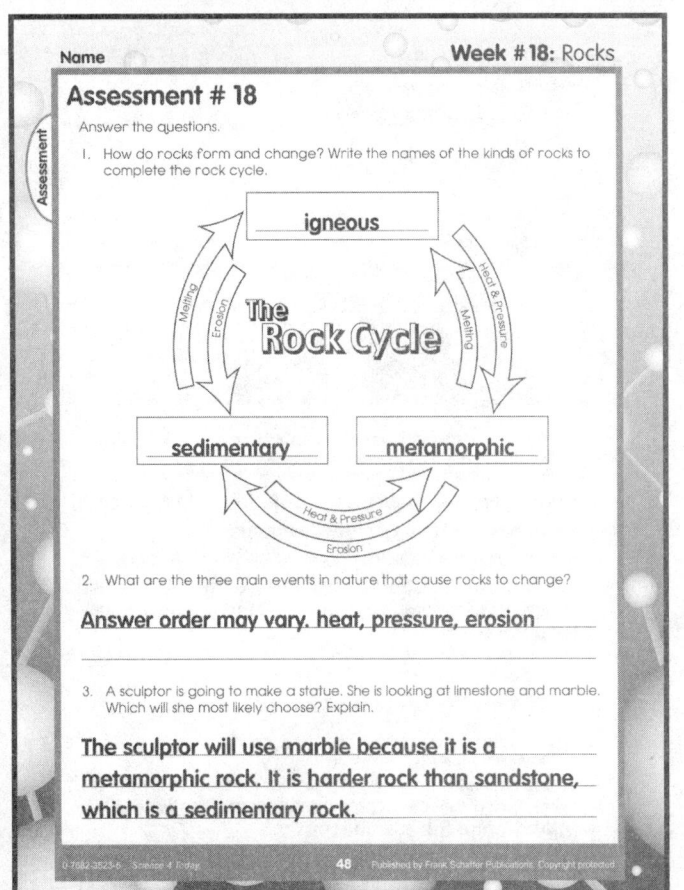

The Rock Cycle: igneous, sedimentary, metamorphic

2. What are the three main events in nature that cause rocks to change?
Answer order may vary. heat, pressure, erosion

3. A sculptor is going to make a statue. She is looking at limestone and marble. Which will she most likely choose? Explain.
The sculptor will use marble because it is a metamorphic rock. It is harder rock than sandstone, which is a sedimentary rock.

Answer Key

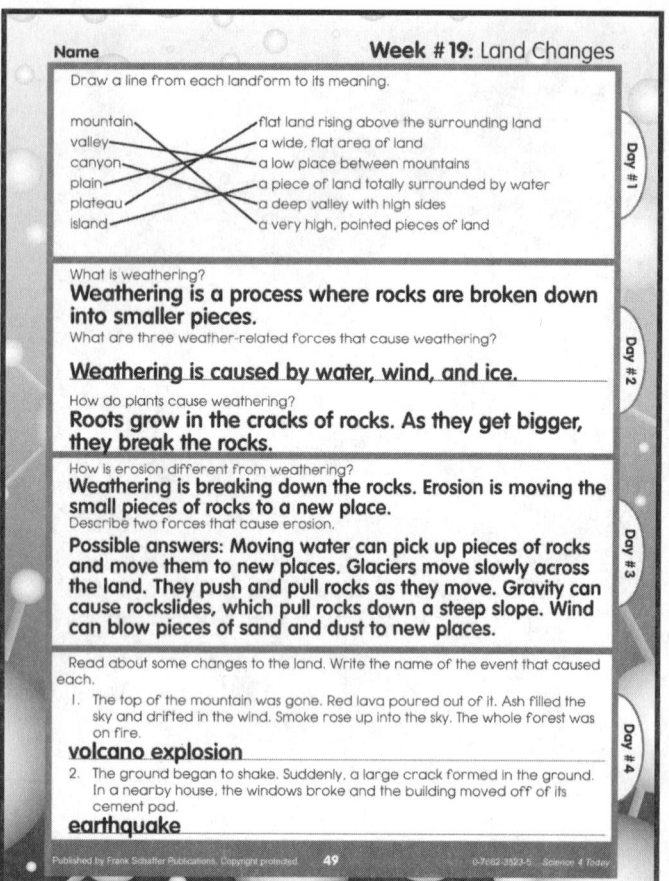

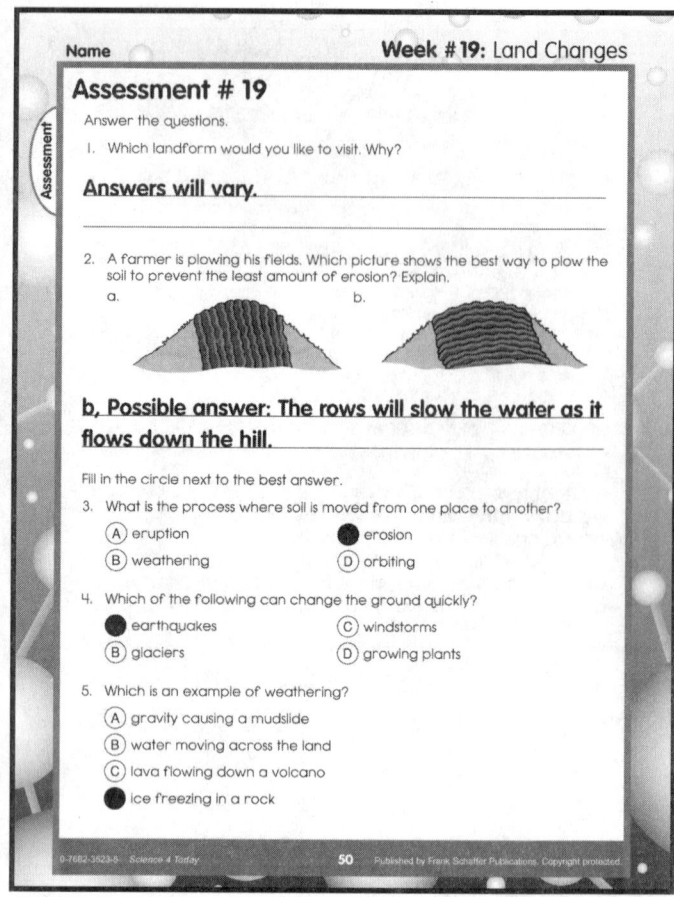

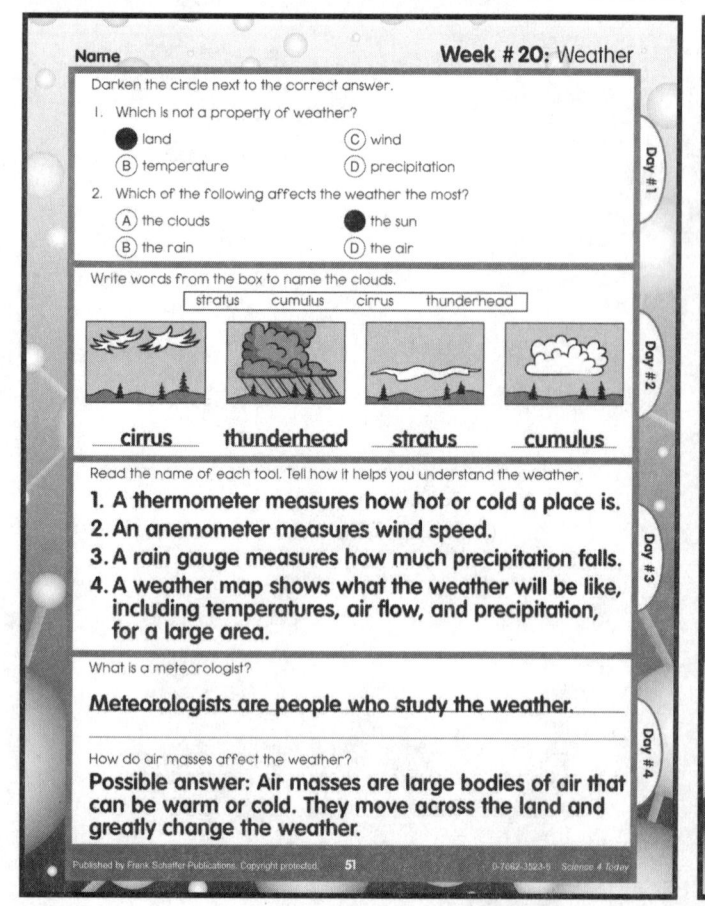

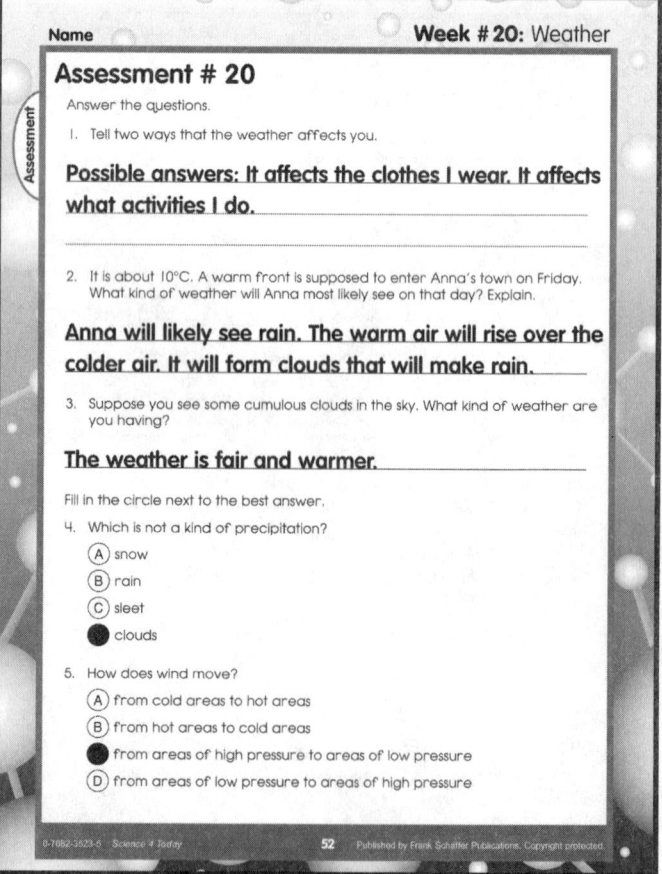

Week #19: Land Changes — Day #1

Draw a line from each landform to its meaning.

- mountain — a very high, pointed pieces of land
- valley — a low place between mountains
- canyon — a deep valley with high sides
- plain — a wide, flat area of land
- plateau — flat land rising above the surrounding land
- island — a piece of land totally surrounded by water

Day #2

What is weathering?
Weathering is a process where rocks are broken down into smaller pieces.

What are three weather-related forces that cause weathering?
Weathering is caused by water, wind, and ice.

How do plants cause weathering?
Roots grow in the cracks of rocks. As they get bigger, they break the rocks.

Day #3

How is erosion different from weathering?
Weathering is breaking down the rocks. Erosion is moving the small pieces of rocks to a new place.

Describe two forces that cause erosion.
Possible answers: Moving water can pick up pieces of rocks and move them to new places. Glaciers move slowly across the land. They push and pull rocks as they move. Gravity can cause rockslides, which pull rocks down a steep slope. Wind can blow pieces of sand and dust to new places.

Day #4

Read about some changes to the land. Write the name of the event that caused each.

1. The top of the mountain was gone. Red lava poured out of it. Ash filled the sky and drifted in the wind. Smoke rose up into the sky. The whole forest was on fire.
volcano explosion

2. The ground began to shake. Suddenly, a large crack formed in the ground. In a nearby house, the windows broke and the building moved off of its cement pad.
earthquake

Week #19: Land Changes — Assessment #19

Answer the questions.

1. Which landform would you like to visit. Why?
Answers will vary.

2. A farmer is plowing his fields. Which picture shows the best way to plow the soil to prevent the least amount of erosion? Explain.
b, Possible answer: The rows will slow the water as it flows down the hill.

Fill in the circle next to the best answer.

3. What is the process where soil is moved from one place to another?
   - A) eruption
   - ● C) erosion
   - B) weathering
   - D) orbiting

4. Which of the following can change the ground quickly?
   - ● A) earthquakes
   - C) windstorms
   - B) glaciers
   - D) growing plants

5. Which is an example of weathering?
   - A) gravity causing a mudslide
   - B) water moving across the land
   - C) lava flowing down a volcano
   - ● D) ice freezing in a rock

Week #20: Weather — Day #1

Darken the circle next to the correct answer.

1. Which is not a property of weather?
   - ● A) land
   - C) wind
   - B) temperature
   - D) precipitation

2. Which of the following affects the weather the most?
   - A) the clouds
   - ● C) the sun
   - B) the rain
   - D) the air

Day #2

Write words from the box to name the clouds.
stratus   cumulus   cirrus   thunderhead

cirrus   thunderhead   stratus   cumulus

Day #3

Read the name of each tool. Tell how it helps you understand the weather.

1. **A thermometer measures how hot or cold a place is.**
2. **An anemometer measures wind speed.**
3. **A rain gauge measures how much precipitation falls.**
4. **A weather map shows what the weather will be like, including temperatures, air flow, and precipitation, for a large area.**

Day #4

What is a meteorologist?
Meteorologists are people who study the weather.

How do air masses affect the weather?
Possible answer: Air masses are large bodies of air that can be warm or cold. They move across the land and greatly change the weather.

Week #20: Weather — Assessment #20

Answer the questions.

1. Tell two ways that the weather affects you.
Possible answers: It affects the clothes I wear. It affects what activities I do.

2. It is about 10°C. A warm front is supposed to enter Anna's town on Friday. What kind of weather will Anna most likely see on that day? Explain.
Anna will likely see rain. The warm air will rise over the colder air. It will form clouds that will make rain.

3. Suppose you see some cumulous clouds in the sky. What kind of weather are you having?
The weather is fair and warmer.

Fill in the circle next to the best answer.

4. Which is not a kind of precipitation?
   - A) snow
   - B) rain
   - C) sleet
   - ● D) clouds

5. How does wind move?
   - A) from cold areas to hot areas
   - B) from hot areas to cold areas
   - ● C) from areas of high pressure to areas of low pressure
   - D) from areas of low pressure to areas of high pressure

Answer Key

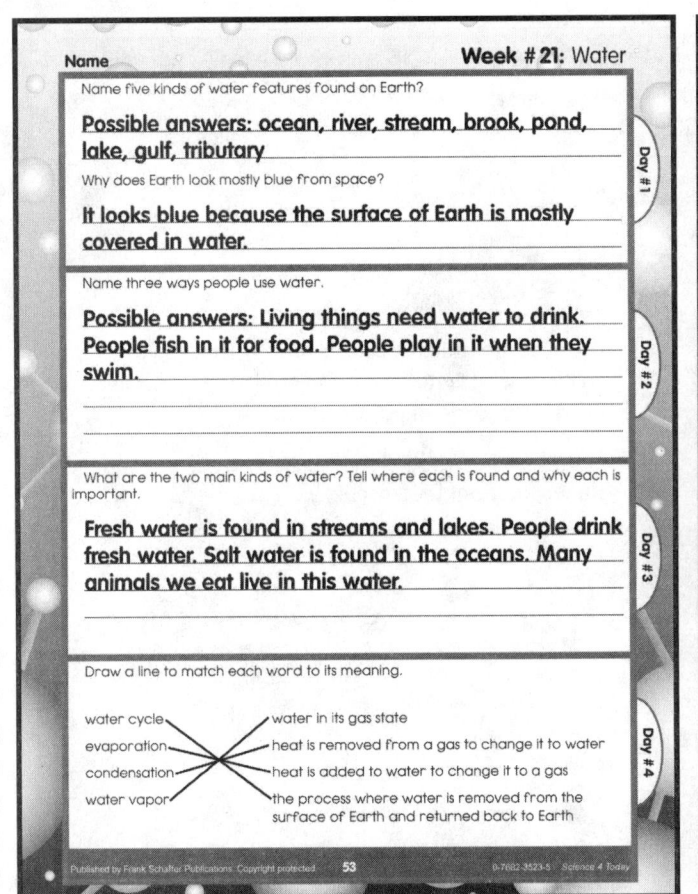

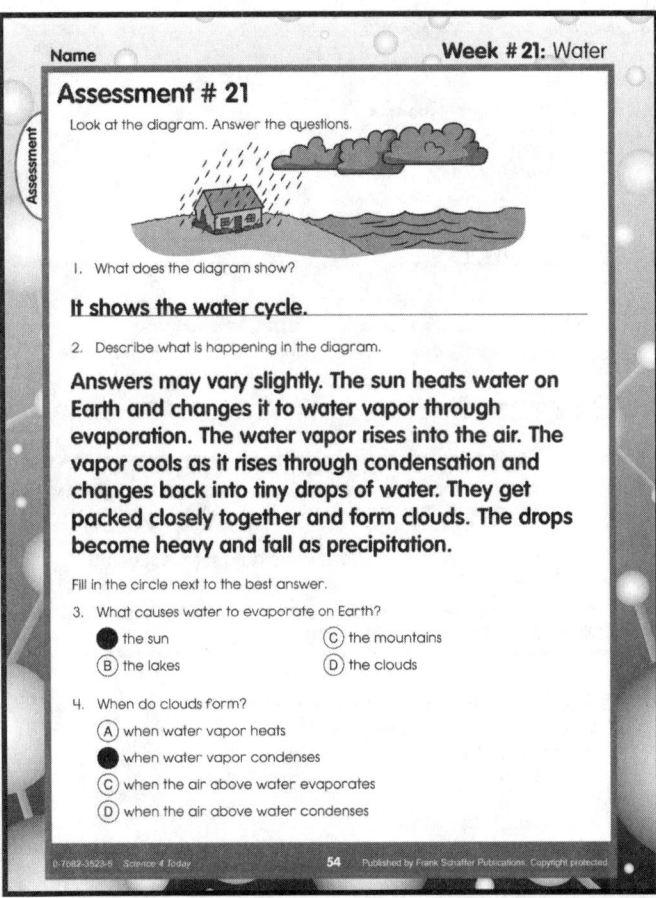

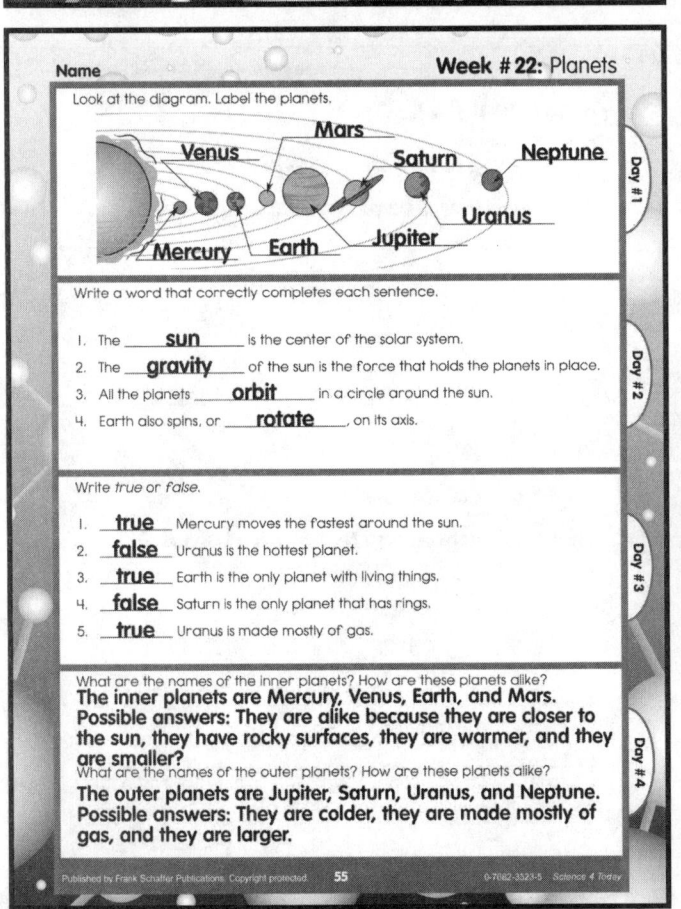

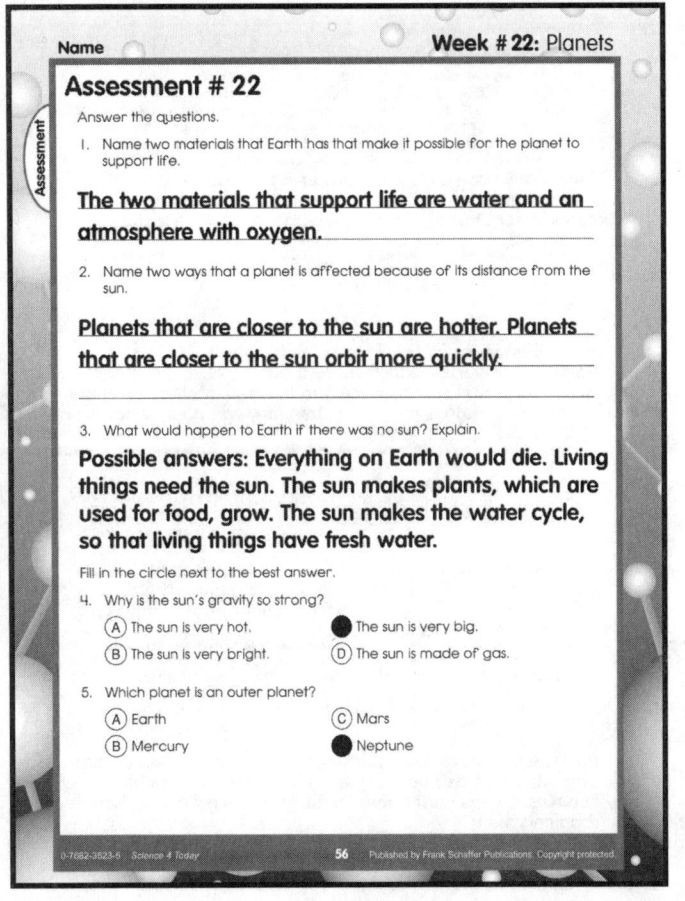

Week #21: Water — Day #1–#4

Name five kinds of water features found on Earth?
Possible answers: ocean, river, stream, brook, pond, lake, gulf, tributary

Why does Earth look mostly blue from space?
It looks blue because the surface of Earth is mostly covered in water.

Name three ways people use water.
Possible answers: Living things need water to drink. People fish in it for food. People play in it when they swim.

What are the two main kinds of water? Tell where each is found and why each is important.
Fresh water is found in streams and lakes. People drink fresh water. Salt water is found in the oceans. Many animals we eat live in this water.

Draw a line to match each word to its meaning.
- water cycle — the process where water is removed from the surface of Earth and returned back to Earth
- evaporation — heat is added to water to change it to a gas
- condensation — heat is removed from a gas to change it to water
- water vapor — water in its gas state

Week #21: Water — Assessment #21

1. What does the diagram show?
   It shows the water cycle.

2. Describe what is happening in the diagram.
   Answers may vary slightly. The sun heats water on Earth and changes it to water vapor through evaporation. The water vapor rises into the air. The vapor cools as it rises through condensation and changes back into tiny drops of water. They get packed closely together and form clouds. The drops become heavy and fall as precipitation.

3. What causes water to evaporate on Earth?
   ● A the sun
   ○ B the lakes
   ○ C the mountains
   ○ D the clouds

4. When do clouds form?
   ○ A when water vapor heats
   ● B when water vapor condenses
   ○ C when the air above water evaporates
   ○ D when the air above water condenses

Week #22: Planets — Day #1–#4

Label the planets: Mercury, Venus, Earth, Mars, Jupiter, Saturn, Uranus, Neptune

Write a word that correctly completes each sentence.
1. The **sun** is the center of the solar system.
2. The **gravity** of the sun is the force that holds the planets in place.
3. All the planets **orbit** in a circle around the sun.
4. Earth also spins, or **rotate**, on its axis.

Write true or false.
1. **true** Mercury moves the fastest around the sun.
2. **false** Uranus is the hottest planet.
3. **true** Earth is the only planet with living things.
4. **false** Saturn is the only planet that has rings.
5. **true** Uranus is made mostly of gas.

What are the names of the inner planets? How are these planets alike?
The inner planets are Mercury, Venus, Earth, and Mars. Possible answers: They are alike because they are closer to the sun, they have rocky surfaces, they are warmer, and they are smaller?

What are the names of the outer planets? How are these planets alike?
The outer planets are Jupiter, Saturn, Uranus, and Neptune. Possible answers: They are colder, they are made mostly of gas, and they are larger.

Week #22: Planets — Assessment #22

1. Name two materials that Earth has that make it possible for the planet to support life.
   The two materials that support life are water and an atmosphere with oxygen.

2. Name two ways that a planet is affected because of its distance from the sun.
   Planets that are closer to the sun are hotter. Planets that are closer to the sun orbit more quickly.

3. What would happen to Earth if there was no sun? Explain.
   Possible answers: Everything on Earth would die. Living things need the sun. The sun makes plants, which are used for food, grow. The sun makes the water cycle, so that living things have fresh water.

4. Why is the sun's gravity so strong?
   ○ A The sun is very hot.
   ○ B The sun is very bright.
   ● C The sun is very big.
   ○ D The sun is made of gas.

5. Which planet is an outer planet?
   ○ A Earth
   ○ B Mercury
   ○ C Mars
   ● D Neptune

Answer Key

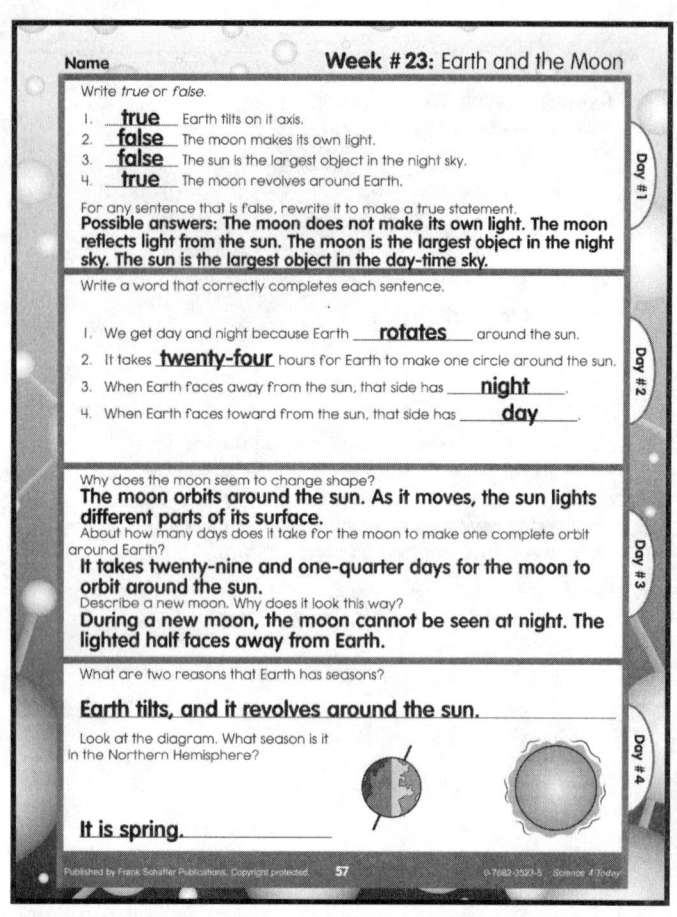

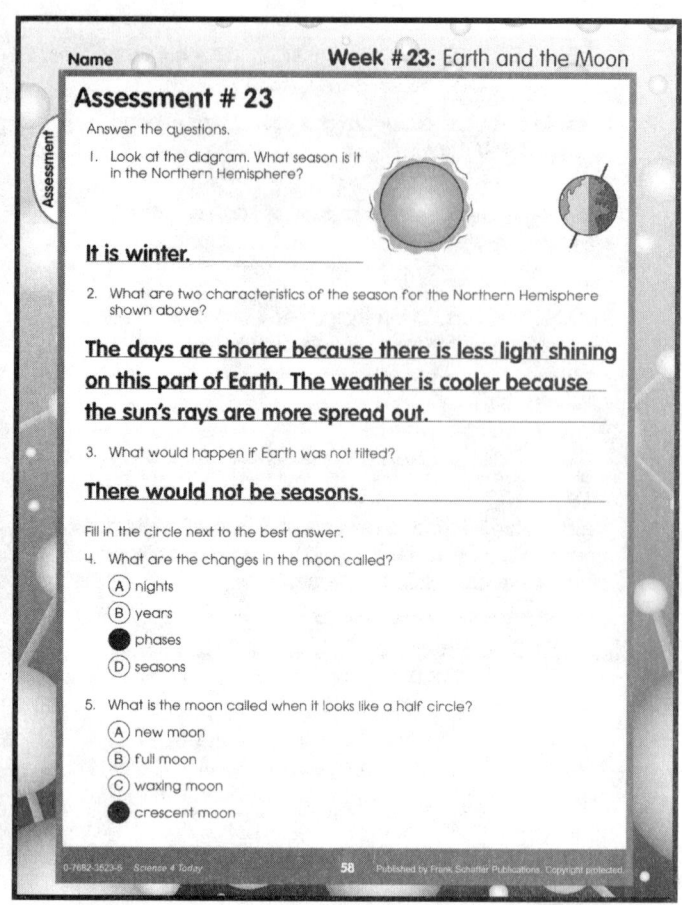

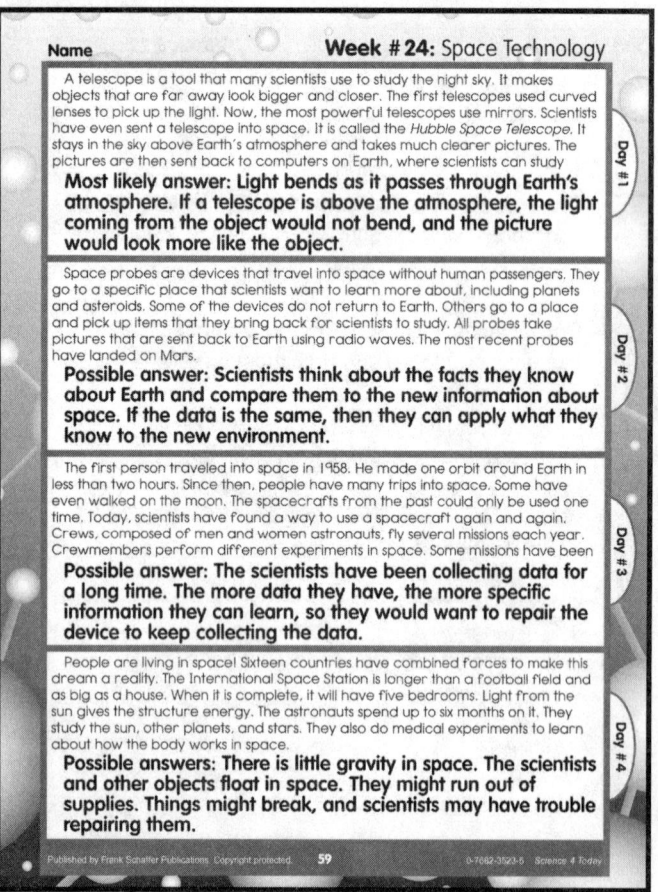

Week #23: Earth and the Moon

Write true or false.
1. **true** Earth tilts on it axis.
2. **false** The moon makes its own light.
3. **false** The sun is the largest object in the night sky.
4. **true** The moon revolves around Earth.

For any sentence that is false, rewrite it to make a true statement.
Possible answers: The moon does not make its own light. The moon reflects light from the sun. The moon is the largest object in the night sky. The sun is the largest object in the day-time sky.

Write a word that correctly completes each sentence.
1. We get day and night because Earth **rotates** around the sun.
2. It takes **twenty-four** hours for Earth to make one circle around the sun.
3. When Earth faces away from the sun, that side has **night**.
4. When Earth faces toward from the sun, that side has **day**.

Why does the moon seem to change shape?
The moon orbits around the sun. As it moves, the sun lights different parts of its surface.

About how many days does it take for the moon to make one complete orbit around Earth?
It takes twenty-nine and one-quarter days for the moon to orbit around the sun.

Describe a new moon. Why does it look this way?
During a new moon, the moon cannot be seen at night. The lighted half faces away from Earth.

What are two reasons that Earth has seasons?
Earth tilts, and it revolves around the sun.

Look at the diagram. What season is it in the Northern Hemisphere?
It is spring.

Assessment #23

Answer the questions.
1. Look at the diagram. What season is it in the Northern Hemisphere?

It is winter.

2. What are two characteristics of the season for the Northern Hemisphere shown above?

The days are shorter because there is less light shining on this part of Earth. The weather is cooler because the sun's rays are more spread out.

3. What would happen if Earth was not tilted?

There would not be seasons.

Fill in the circle next to the best answer.
4. What are the changes in the moon called?
  A) nights
  B) years
  ● phases
  D) seasons

5. What is the moon called when it looks like a half circle?
  A) new moon
  B) full moon
  C) waxing moon
  ● crescent moon

Week #24: Space Technology

A telescope is a tool that many scientists use to study the night sky. It makes objects that are far away look bigger and closer. The first telescopes used curved lenses to pick up the light. Now, the most powerful telescopes use mirrors. Scientists have even sent a telescope into space. It is called the *Hubble Space Telescope*. It stays in the sky above Earth's atmosphere and takes much clearer pictures. The pictures are then sent back to computers on Earth, where scientists can study
Most likely answer: Light bends as it passes through Earth's atmosphere. If a telescope is above the atmosphere, the light coming from the object would not bend, and the picture would look more like the object.

Space probes are devices that travel into space without human passengers. They go to a specific place that scientists want to learn more about, including planets and asteroids. Some of the devices do not return to Earth. Others go to a place and pick up items that they bring back for scientists to study. All probes take pictures that are sent back to Earth using radio waves. The most recent probes have landed on Mars.
Possible answer: Scientists think about the facts they know about Earth and compare them to the new information about space. If the data is the same, then they can apply what they know to the new environment.

The first person traveled into space in 1958. He made one orbit around Earth in less than two hours. Since then, people have many trips into space. Some have even walked on the moon. The spacecrafts from the past could only be used one time. Today, scientists have found a way to use a spacecraft again and again. Crews, composed of men and women astronauts, fly several missions each year. Crewmembers perform different experiments in space. Some missions have been
Possible answer: The scientists have been collecting data for a long time. The more data they have, the more specific information they can learn, so they would want to repair the device to keep collecting the data.

People are living in space! Sixteen countries have combined forces to make this dream a reality. The International Space Station is longer than a football field and as big as a house. When it is complete, it will have five bedrooms. Light from the sun gives the structure energy. The astronauts spend up to six months on it. They study the sun, other planets, and stars. They also do medical experiments to learn about how the body works in space.
Possible answers: There is little gravity in space. The scientists and other objects float in space. They might run out of supplies. Things might break, and astronauts may have trouble repairing them.

Assessment #24

Answer the questions.
How has technology helped us learn about the solar system?
Answer will vary. Accept reasonable answers.

Would you like to travel in space? Why or why not?
Answer will vary. Accept reasonable answers.

Answer Key

Week #25: Energy Technology

Day #1

In some places, the wind is a constant force. Scientists have found a way to convert it into electricity. Giant turbines are built up above the ground. The turbines have blades on them. As the wind blows, it turns the blades and spins the turbine. The turbine powers a generator, which produces electricity.

Why are the turbines built high above the ground?

The wind is more constant and more forceful farther above the Earth's surface.

Day #2

Moving water has energy. People long ago used water energy to turn large rock wheels to grind corn and wheat into flour. People still use water energy today. They build large dams to hold water in lakes. When the water is released, it turns large turbines. The turbines power generators, which produce electric energy. The electricity moves through power lines to light and heat buildings.

Is it possible for all electricity to be powered by water? Why or why not?

Not all power can come from water because there are many places on Earth that do not have access to lots of water.

Day #3

Solar energy is energy that comes from the sun. Some people use solar energy to heat their houses. Flat, black panels on the roof gather the light. The panels have water-filled tubes inside. The water in these tubes gets hot and travels to a heat exchanger, filled with more water. The heat from the water-filled tubes is transferred to the water in the heat exchanger. The hot water moves through a special heating system to warm a house.

Why are the panels on the roof black?

The color black absorbs the most light and would better heat the water.

Day #4

To make nuclear energy, scientists break an atom's nucleus, which creates heat. The heat is converted into steam. Steam powers machines that make electricity. Nuclear energy is good because it does not use fossil fuels, like coal. It does not release pollutants into the air, either. However, the fuel used to split the atoms, uranium, is dangerous once it is used. It must be removed and stored away from living things.

Fuels that power many power plants are running out. Since atoms are the main source of energy in nuclear energy, they will not run out.

Assessment #25 — Week #25: Energy Technology

Answer the questions.

1. Why is wind a good source of energy? Why might it be a bad source of energy?

Possible answers: Wind is a good source of energy because it is an inexhaustible resource that cannot be used up. It might not blow all the time, which might keep the generators from producing electricity, which people depend on.

2. Would a homeowner living in Florida or Alaska be more likely to use solar heating? Explain.

Possible answers: A homeowner living in Florida would be more likely to use solar power because the sun shines more often there. The heat would be constant. Alaska has periods of little light, so the water would not stay hot. Also, snow might cover the panels, so no light could be collected.

3. Other than energy, what are some other benefits of a town building a dam?

Possible answers: People use them for fun activities, such as boating, swimming, and fishing. They provide a habitat for water plants and animals to live.

4. Which form of energy do you think is the best for people to use? Give two reasons in your explanation.

Answers will vary.

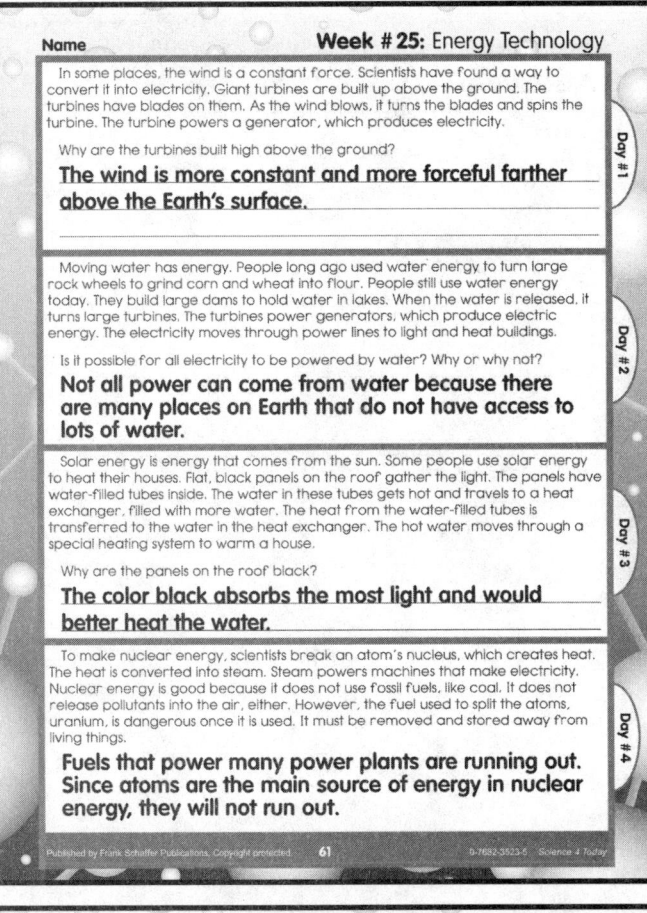

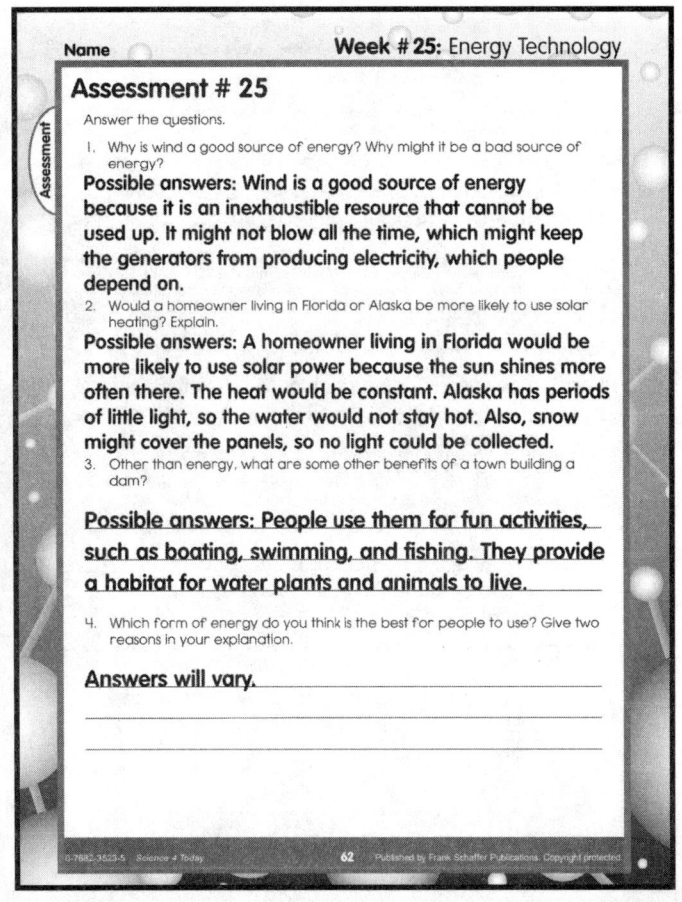

Week #26: Medical Technology

Day #1

The body has many organs, or body parts, that work together. However, many of these parts are inside and covered up by skin. Sometimes, doctors need to look at these parts if you get sick or hurt. They will use a machine called a *CT machine*. The machine works like a camera. It takes pictures that are like x-rays. A doctor can look at the pictures and quickly see if you are bleeding inside or if something unusual is growing.

Possible answers: The doctor can find out quickly what is wrong with the body. The scans look inside without opening the body or causing pain.

Day #2

You eat food and digest it to give you energy. There are many parts that make the process work smoothly. However, sometimes the kidneys do not work. The kidneys are the body parts that remove the wastes from your blood. Luckily, there is a machine to help these people. A dialyzer acts like the kidneys. A nurse attaches some tubes to the sick person. The machine pulls the blood out, cleans the wastes out of it, and returns the blood through another tube. It takes about four hours and must be done three times each week.

How does the dialyzer act like a kidney?

The dialyzer cleans the body of wastes like a kidney does.

Day #3

Some people can't see things that are close. Others can't see things that are far away. Glasses often correct these problems. Lasers also help people who cannot see things clearly. A laser is a slim, but powerful beam of light. The light makes a cut by burning where it lands. In this case, the beam of light cuts the top layer of the eye. The eye changes shape where it is cut. This kind of surgery is safer than using a knife, and people can use their eyes the next day.

How is a laser like a knife?

The laser can cut like a knife.

Day #4

Jon Comer is a professional skateboarder. He drops into a half-pipe and does many amazing tricks. What is really amazing is that Comer has a prosthetic—an artificial limb—for one leg! Scientists join technology and science to help many people like Comer. The limbs are made of plastic and look real. When joined to the body, muscle movement is changed to electric signals, which makes the artificial limb move.

How do prosthetics help people who are missing limbs?

Possible answer: People with prosthetics can move and do things just like if they have not lost a body part.

Assessment #26 — Week #26: Medical Technology

Draw lines to match each word with its meaning.

- technology → machines and activities that are used to help people
- prosthetics → plastic parts that take the place of missing body parts
- CT machine → a machine that takes pictures of the inside of the body
- laser → a high-powered beam of light that cuts by burning
- dialyzer → a machine that cleans the blood of wastes

Answer the question.

Why is it important that science and technology work together?

Answers will vary.

Answer Key

Week #27: Farm Technology

Long ago, farmers used hand tools, like hoes, to break the soil before they planted seeds. Then, they spread the seeds and harvested the crops by hand. In the 1800s, farmers used iron plows pulled by horses to break the soil. They still spread seed and harvested the crops by hand, though.

How do you think a plow made farming easier?

Possible answers: A plow was faster. Since an animal pulled the tool, it took less physical work for the farmer.

By 1930, farmers used tractors to pull a plow. They also used a harrow to break up big chunks of dirt. Finally, a combine cut and harvested the crop. Where as it took about 32 hours each week in the 1800s to farm an acre, now it took a farmer about 8 hours to do the same work.

How did the new technology help farmers in the 1930s?

Possible answers: They had more tools, so they did not have to do everything by hand. It was probably easier. It was also faster.

Today, a farmer can plow a field in about an hour. Moreover, a person with a small farm can buy one tractor and different implements, or tools, to do all the jobs, from plowing to harvesting. Some tractors even have air conditioning.

How might a farmer benefit by buying one tractor and different tools?

Possible answers: It is cheaper to buy one main machine and some tools rather than buy many different machines.

Is farming easier today than it was a hundred years ago? Explain.

Possible answer: Yes, farming is easier today. New kinds of farm tools help get the job done more easily and quickly.

Assessment #27: Farm Technology

How has technology changed farming? Use the words below in your paragraph.

| plow | tractor | machine | technology |

Answers will vary.

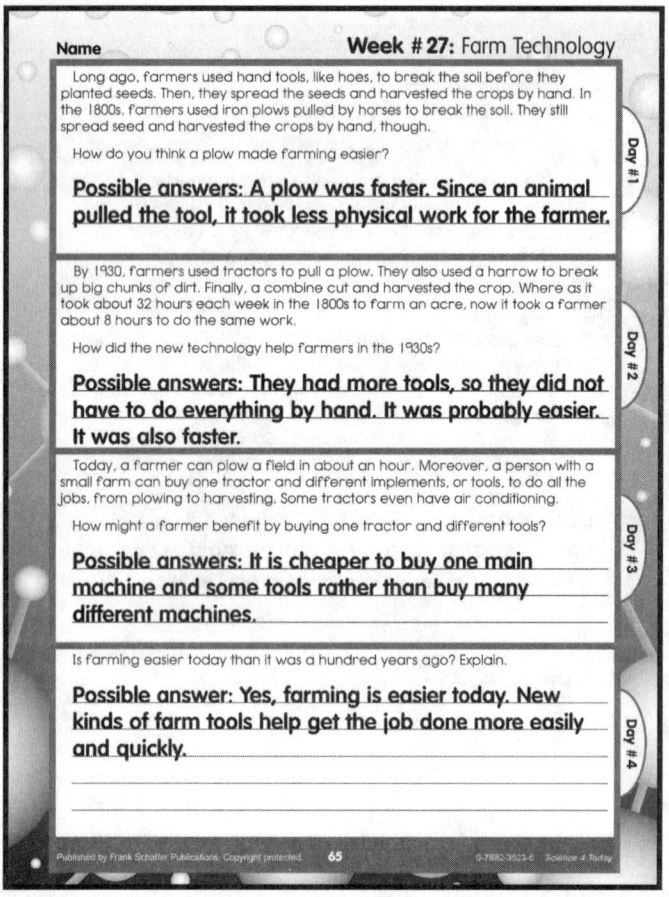

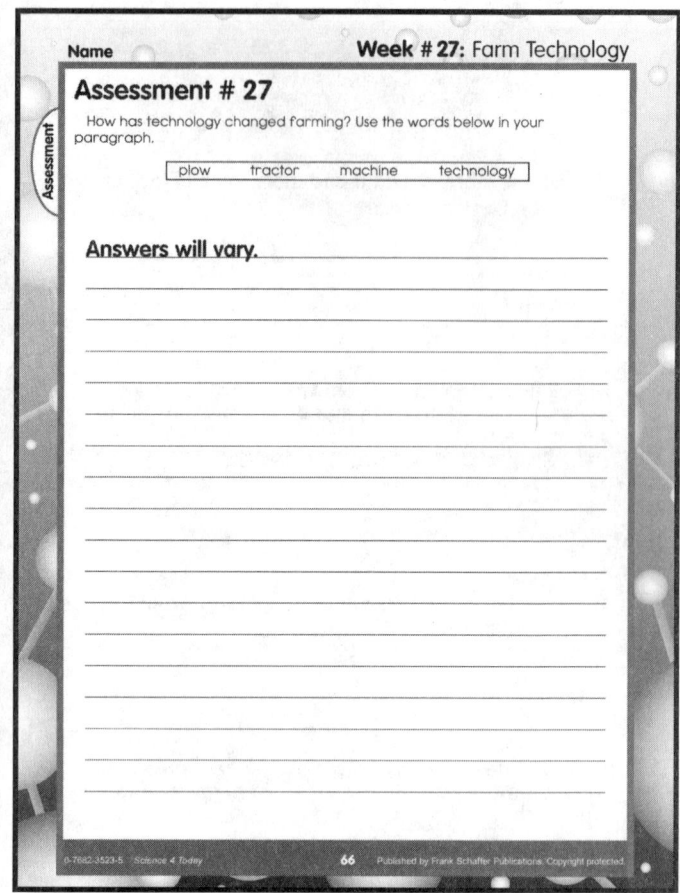

Week #28: Computer Technology

What is a computer?
A computer is a device that can store information and work to solve problems very quickly in a process that makes sense.

An abacus was a tool that merchants used to calculate numbers in ancient China. Many people think it is the first computer. Why?
Possible answer: An abacus was used to add and subtract. It solved problems very quickly in a way that made sense.

Draw a line to match each word with its meaning.
- monitor — the part where people see the information
- keyboard — the part on which people input the information
- file — the smallest unit in which information is stored
- microprocessor — the part that does the computing
- Internet — the network that links computers all over the world
- software — a program that makes the computer work
- memory chip — the part that stores all the information

Name four ways that people use a computer to communicate.

Possible answers: email, blogs, personal Web sites, cameras, microphones

Why is a digital camera a kind of computer?

Possible answers: It stores information. It has a screen to view pictures. It has a microprocessor and memory. It needs software to make it work.

Assessment #28: Computer Technology

How have computers changed society? Use the words from the box in your paragraph.

| work | play | learn | communicate |

Answers will vary.

Answer Key

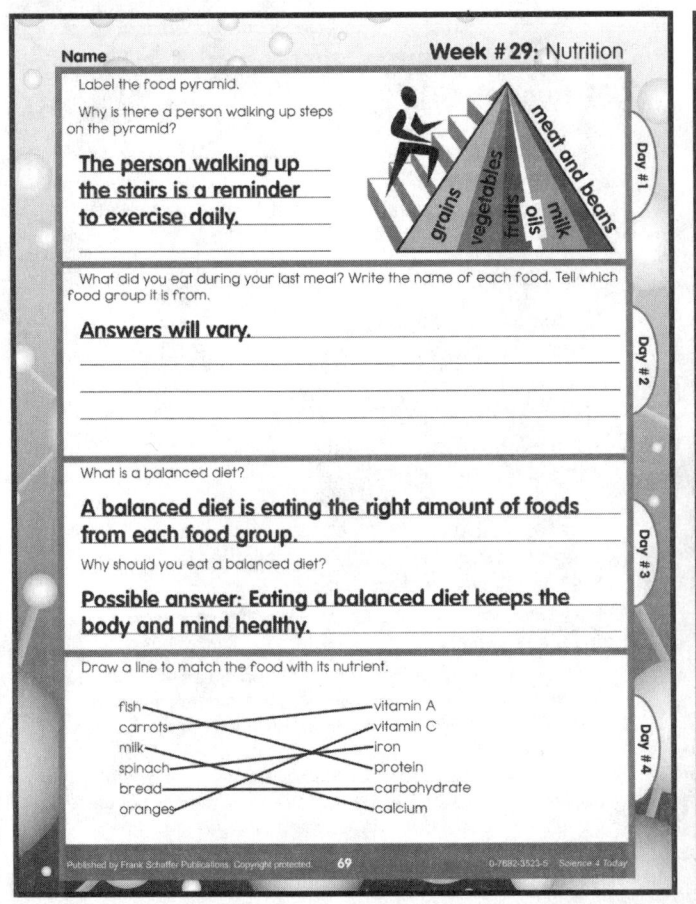

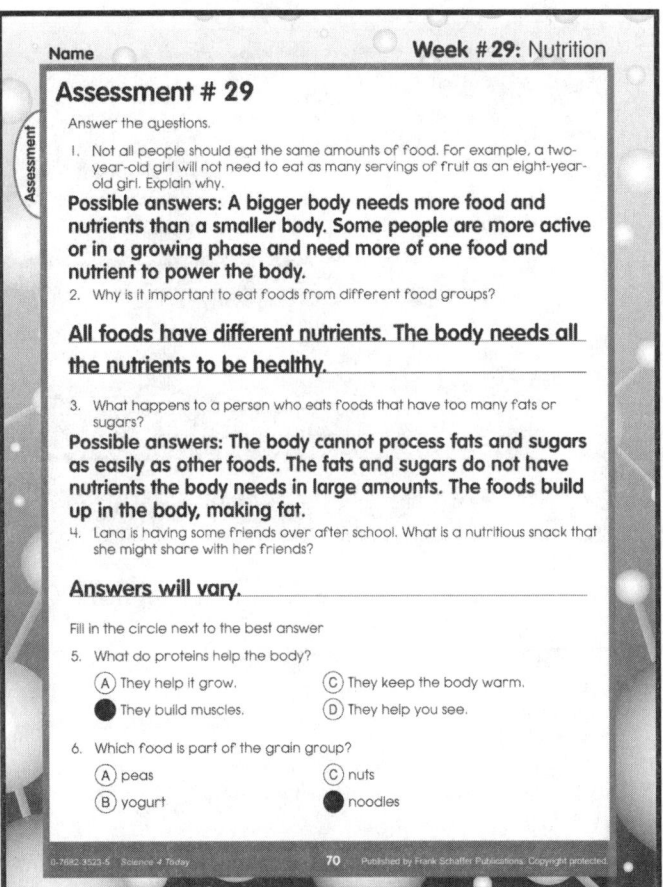

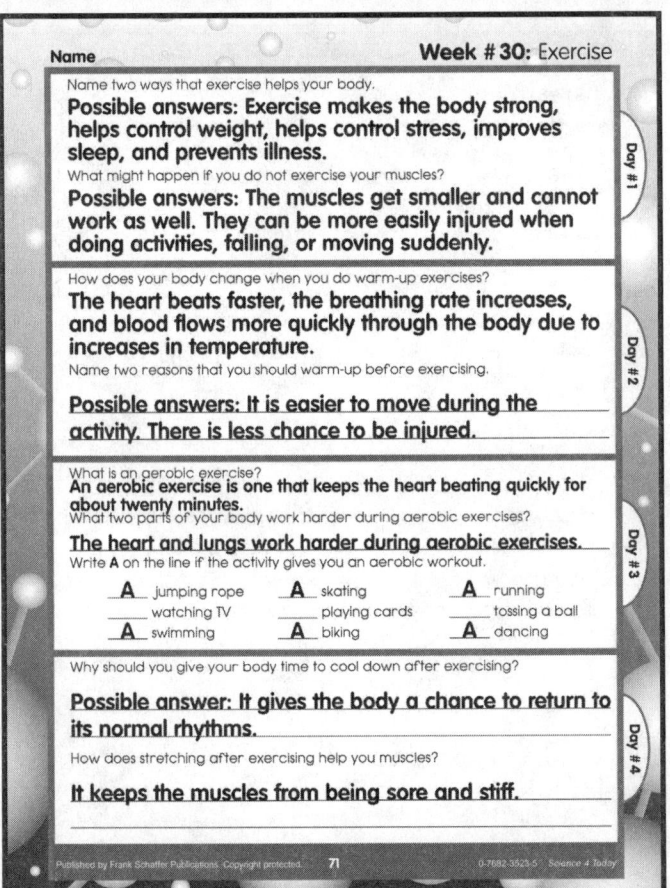

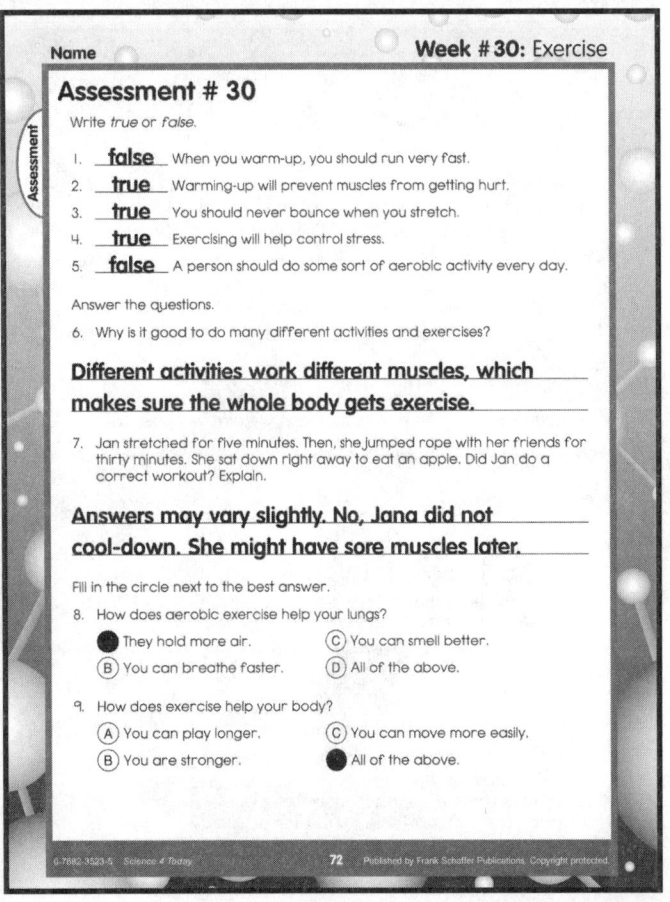

Name **Week # 29:** Nutrition

Day #1

Label the food pyramid.

Why is there a person walking up steps on the pyramid?

The person walking up the stairs is a reminder to exercise daily.

grains
vegetables
fruits
oils
milk
meat and beans

Day #2

What did you eat during your last meal? Write the name of each food. Tell which food group it is from.

Answers will vary.

Day #3

What is a balanced diet?

A balanced diet is eating the right amount of foods from each food group.

Why should you eat a balanced diet?

Possible answer: Eating a balanced diet keeps the body and mind healthy.

Day #4

Draw a line to match the food with its nutrient.

Food	Nutrient
fish	protein
carrots	vitamin A
milk	calcium
spinach	iron
bread	carbohydrate
oranges	vitamin C

Published by Frank Schaffer Publications. Copyright protected. 69 0-7682-3523-5 *Science 4 Today*

Name **Week # 29:** Nutrition

Assessment # 29

Assessment

Answer the questions.

1. Not all people should eat the same amounts of food. For example, a two-year-old girl will not need to eat as many servings of fruit as an eight-year-old girl. Explain why.
Possible answers: A bigger body needs more food and nutrients than a smaller body. Some people are more active or in a growing phase and need more of one food and nutrient to power the body.
2. Why is it important to eat foods from different food groups?
All foods have different nutrients. The body needs all the nutrients to be healthy.
3. What happens to a person who eats foods that have too many fats or sugars?
Possible answers: The body cannot process fats and sugars as easily as other foods. The fats and sugars do not have nutrients the body needs in large amounts. The foods build up in the body, making fat.
4. Lana is having some friends over after school. What is a nutritious snack that she might share with her friends?
Answers will vary.

Fill in the circle next to the best answer.

5. What do proteins help the body?
   - (A) They help it grow.
   - ● They build muscles.
   - (C) They keep the body warm.
   - (D) They help you see.
6. Which food is part of the grain group?
   - (A) peas
   - (B) yogurt
   - (C) nuts
   - ● noodles

0-7682-3523-5 *Science 4 Today* 70 Published by Frank Schaffer Publications. Copyright protected.

Name **Week # 30:** Exercise

Day #1

Name two ways that exercise helps your body.

Possible answers: Exercise makes the body strong, helps control weight, helps control stress, improves sleep, and prevents illness.

What might happen if you do not exercise your muscles?

Possible answers: The muscles get smaller and cannot work as well. They can be more easily injured when doing activities, falling, or moving suddenly.

Day #2

How does your body change when you do warm-up exercises?

The heart beats faster, the breathing rate increases, and blood flows more quickly through the body due to increases in temperature.

Name two reasons that you should warm-up before exercising.

Possible answers: It is easier to move during the activity. There is less chance to be injured.

Day #3

What is an aerobic exercise?

An aerobic exercise is one that keeps the heart beating quickly for about twenty minutes.

What two parts of your body work harder during aerobic exercises?

The heart and lungs work harder during aerobic exercises.

Write **A** on the line if the activity gives you an aerobic workout.

A jumping rope	**A** skating	**A** running
____ watching TV	____ playing cards	____ tossing a ball
A swimming	**A** biking	**A** dancing

Day #4

Why should you give your body time to cool down after exercising?

Possible answer: It gives the body a chance to return to its normal rhythms.

How does stretching after exercising help you muscles?

It keeps the muscles from being sore and stiff.

Published by Frank Schaffer Publications. Copyright protected. 71 0-7682-3523-5 *Science 4 Today*

Name **Week # 30:** Exercise

Assessment # 30

Assessment

Write *true* or *false*.

1. **false** When you warm-up, you should run very fast.
2. **true** Warming-up will prevent muscles from getting hurt.
3. **true** You should never bounce when you stretch.
4. **true** Exercising will help control stress.
5. **false** A person should do some sort of aerobic activity every day.

Answer the questions.

6. Why is it good to do many different activities and exercises?
Different activities work different muscles, which makes sure the whole body gets exercise.
7. Jan stretched for five minutes. Then, she jumped rope with her friends for thirty minutes. She sat down right away to eat an apple. Did Jan do a correct workout? Explain.
Answers may vary slightly. No, Jana did not cool-down. She might have sore muscles later.

Fill in the circle next to the best answer.

8. How does aerobic exercise help your lungs?
   - ● They hold more air.
   - (B) You can breathe faster.
   - (C) You can smell better.
   - (D) All of the above.
9. How does exercise help your body?
   - (A) You can play longer.
   - (B) You are stronger.
   - (C) You can move more easily.
   - ● All of the above.

0-7682-3523-5 *Science 4 Today* 72 Published by Frank Schaffer Publications. Copyright protected.

Answer Key

Week #31: Safety

Unscramble the letters in bold to complete the fire safety rules.

1. Put smoke **srcotdeet** near the bedrooms. — **detectors**
2. Make a plan to **speeca** from every room in the house. — **escape**
3. Choose a place where everyone should meet **duostie**. — **outside**
4. Keep a fire **stuigehrnixe** on each floor in the house. — **extinguisher**
5. If your **selocht** catch on fire, you should stop, drop, and roll. — **clothes**

Think about thunderstorm safety. Write true or false.

1. **true** Stay away from glass windows and doors.
2. **false** Stand under a tree if there is lightning.
3. **true** Stay away from water.
4. **true** If you cannot reach shelter, get down on your knees and tuck your head.
5. **false** Stay talking on the phone with an adult.

If you are in a building, what should you do during an earthquake?
Possible answers: Move under a heavy piece of furniture or stand in a doorway. Stay away from glass windows and doors and heavy objects that might fall down.

If you are outside, what should you do during an earthquake?
Possible answers: Move to an open area away from buildings and power lines.

Write words to correctly complete the tornado safety rules.

1. Move to a room that does not have **glass**.
2. If you are outside and cannot reach shelter, move to a **ditch**.
3. Listen to weather **report** on the TV or radio.
4. Stay put until the danger is **gone, over**.

Assessment #31 — Week #31: Safety

Answer the questions.

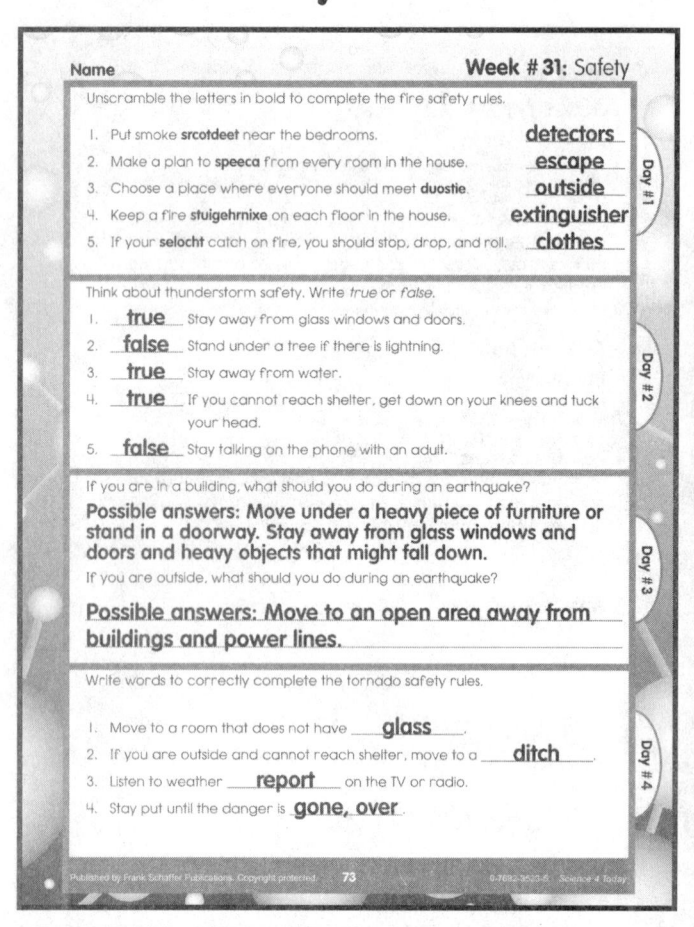

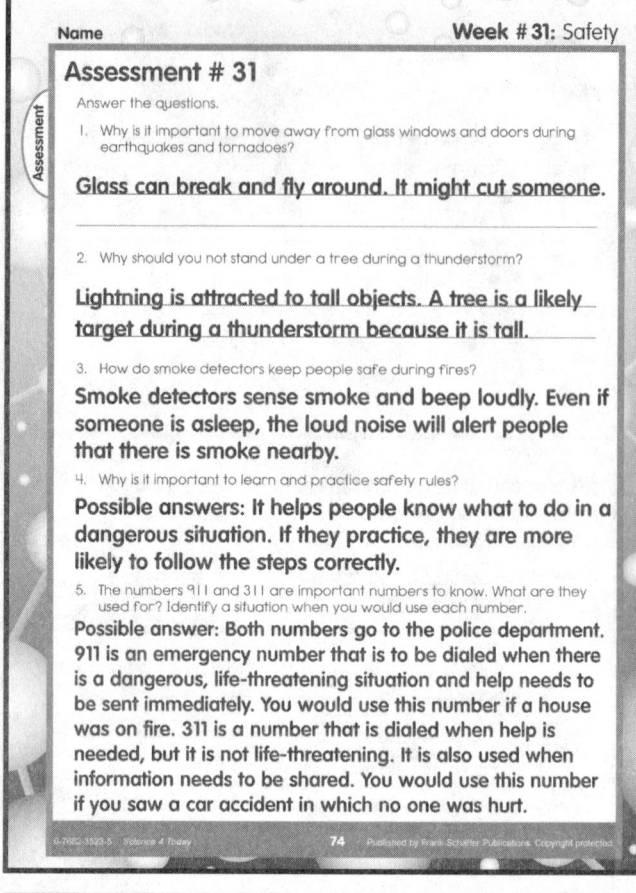

1. Why is it important to move away from glass windows and doors during earthquakes and tornadoes?
Glass can break and fly around. It might cut someone.

2. Why should you not stand under a tree during a thunderstorm?
Lightning is attracted to tall objects. A tree is a likely target during a thunderstorm because it is tall.

3. How do smoke detectors keep people safe during fires?
Smoke detectors sense smoke and beep loudly. Even if someone is asleep, the loud noise will alert people that there is smoke nearby.

4. Why is it important to learn and practice safety rules?
Possible answers: It helps people know what to do in a dangerous situation. If they practice, they are more likely to follow the steps correctly.

5. The numbers 911 and 311 are important numbers to know. What are they used for? Identify a situation when you would use each number.
Possible answer: Both numbers go to the police department. 911 is an emergency number that is to be dialed when there is a dangerous, life-threatening situation and help needs to be sent immediately. You would use this number if a house was on fire. 311 is a number that is dialed when help is needed, but it is not life-threatening. It is also used when information needs to be shared. You would use this number if you saw a car accident in which no one was hurt.

Week #32: Rain Forest Destruction

More than half of all plants and animal species in the world live in the rain forest. Scientists believe that millions more exist, but have not yet been discovered. However, in the last fifty years, nearly half of the rain forests have been destroyed.

Why might scientists be concerned about the loss of the rain forests?
Possible answer: They might be concerned because animals and plants that we do not know are about are dying. They might be important to the balance of the rain forest.

The rain forest is of great interest to many companies. Loggers cut large areas of trees to harvest the wood for a variety of products. Miners strip the land of trees to dig out minerals. The land is left bare once the companies take what they want.

Is it a good idea to leave the land bare? Explain.
Possible answer: It is not a good idea to leave the land bare. Without the plants, wind and water will cause erosion and remove the soil. The land is flat and will easily flood, too.

People have lived in the rain forest for thousands of years. Each year, they burn parts of forest so they can grow crops. So many of them use the slash and burn method that huge clouds of smoke are carried to other continents. Moreover, rain forest soil is thin and does not have many nutrients. After farming the land for several years, the soil no longer grows healthy plants. The people clear more trees to make new fields.

Smoke from the fires cause pollution in other parts of the world. Native people continue to clear land, which removes trees and leaves land bare, resulting in soil erosion.

The native people use the plants in the rain forest for medicines. Drug companies are working with them to find out which plants they use to cure different illnesses. Then, scientists research how to use the plants to make new medicines. For example, the rosy periwinkle, a flower grown in the Madagascar rain forest, is now used to make a drug that helps cancer patients.

How is the relationship between drug companies and native people a positive one?
Possible answer: The drug companies are finding new medicines to help people. The native people are earning money, so they want to keep the forest safe.

Assessment #32 — Week #32: Rain Forest Destruction

Fill in the circle next to the best answer.

1. What is the slash and burn method?
   A. logging companies dig out minerals
   B. workers find and cook food
   ● native people clear land to grow crops
   D. logging companies cut down trees

2. Why is it important to work with the native people living in a rain forest?
   ● They know about the plants and animals.
   B. They want to sell their land.
   C. They don't want strangers in the rain forest.
   D. They want to make money logging.

Write a paragraph telling three reasons why the rain forest is important.

Possible answers: The rain forests provide oxygen, medicines, a variety of animal and plant life, livelihood for the native people, wood products, mineral products, food, adds to the water cycle, controls temperature, and recreational activities.

Answer Key

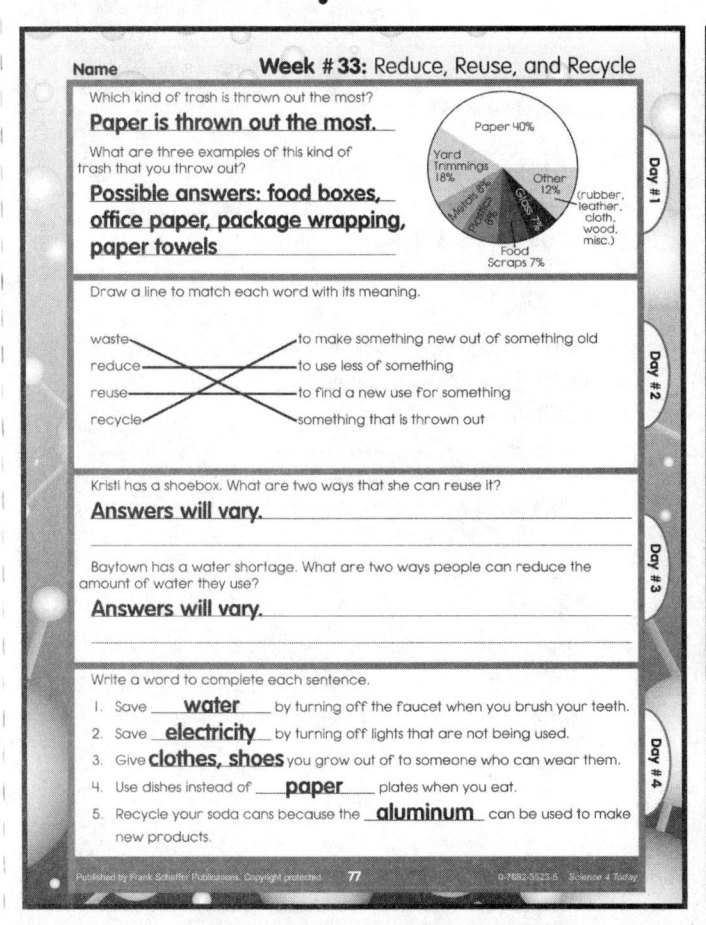

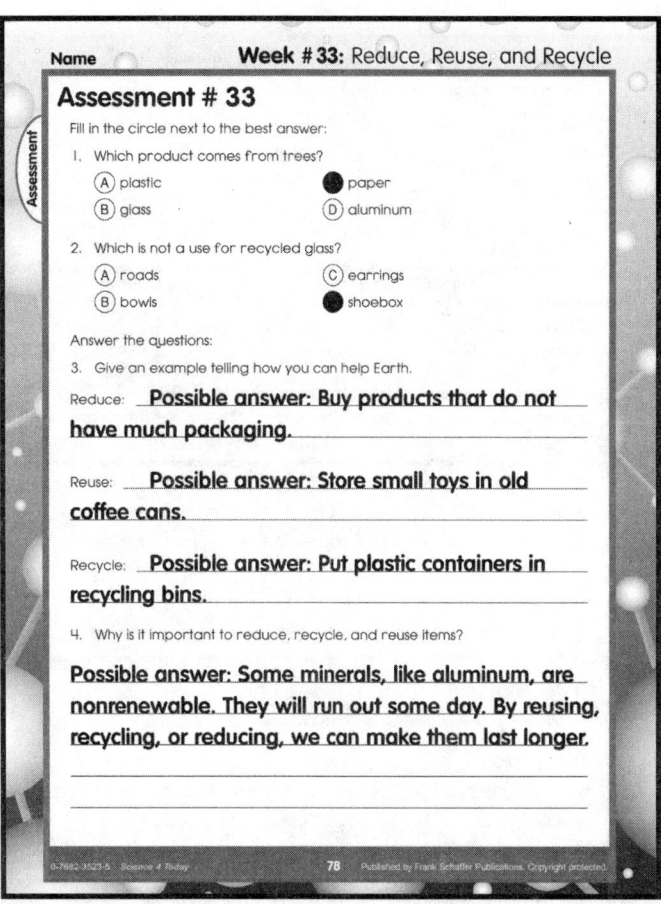

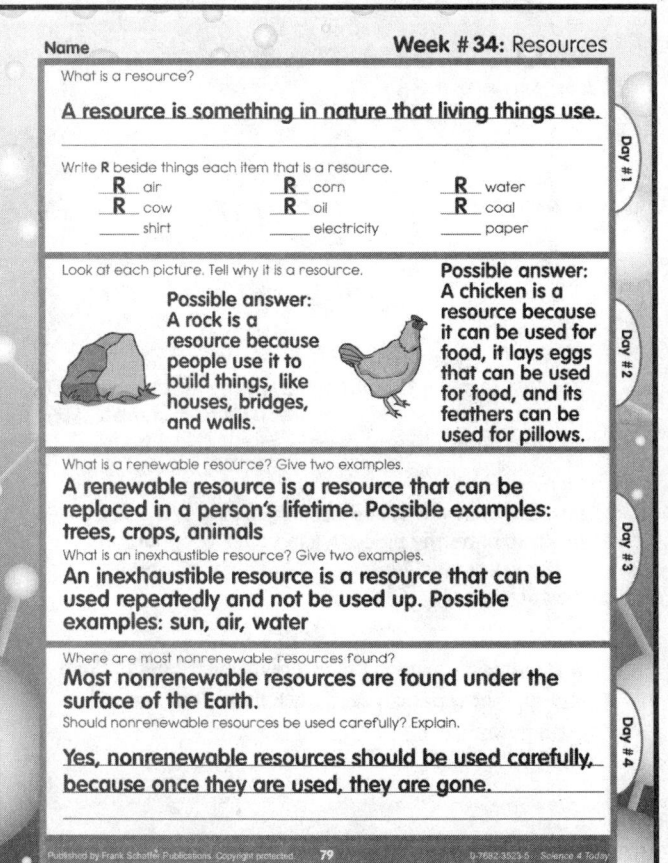

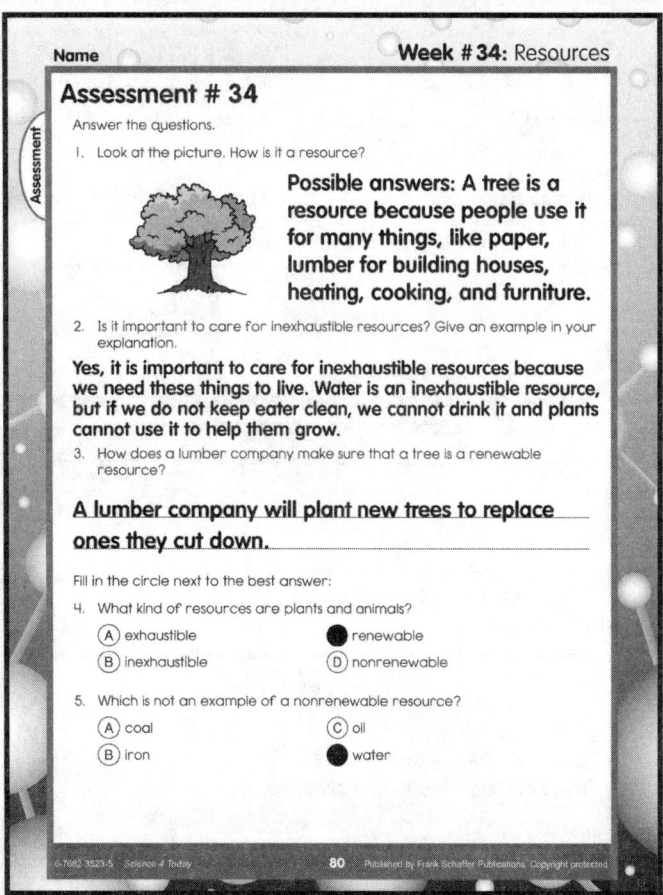

Week #33: Reduce, Reuse, and Recycle

Day #1
Which kind of trash is thrown out the most?
Paper is thrown out the most.
What are three examples of this kind of trash that you throw out?
Possible answers: food boxes, office paper, package wrapping, paper towels

Pie chart: Paper 40%, Yard Trimmings 18%, Other 12% (rubber, leather, cloth, wood, misc.), Food Scraps 7%, Glass 2%, Metals 8%, Plastics 8%

Day #2
Draw a line to match each word with its meaning.
- waste — something that is thrown out
- reduce — to use less of something
- reuse — to find a new use for something
- recycle — to make something new out of something old

Day #3
Kristi has a shoebox. What are two ways that she can reuse it?
Answers will vary.

Baytown has a water shortage. What are two ways people can reduce the amount of water they use?
Answers will vary.

Day #4
Write a word to complete each sentence.
1. Save **water** by turning off the faucet when you brush your teeth.
2. Save **electricity** by turning off lights that are not being used.
3. Give **clothes, shoes** you grow out of to someone who can wear them.
4. Use dishes instead of **paper** plates when you eat.
5. Recycle your soda cans because the **aluminum** can be used to make new products.

Assessment #33 — Week #33: Reduce, Reuse, and Recycle

Fill in the circle next to the best answer:
1. Which product comes from trees?
   A) plastic ● **paper** B) glass D) aluminum
2. Which is not a use for recycled glass?
   A) roads C) earrings B) bowls ● **shoebox**

Answer the questions:
3. Give an example telling how you can help Earth.
   Reduce: **Possible answer: Buy products that do not have much packaging.**
   Reuse: **Possible answer: Store small toys in old coffee cans.**
   Recycle: **Possible answer: Put plastic containers in recycling bins.**

4. Why is it important to reduce, recycle, and reuse items?
   Possible answer: Some minerals, like aluminum, are nonrenewable. They will run out some day. By reusing, recycling, or reducing, we can make them last longer.

Week #34: Resources

Day #1
What is a resource?
A resource is something in nature that living things use.

Write R beside things each item that is a resource.
- R air R corn R water
- R cow R oil R coal
- ___ shirt ___ electricity ___ paper

Day #2
Look at each picture. Tell why it is a resource.
Possible answer: A rock is a resource because people use it to build things, like houses, bridges, and walls.
Possible answer: A chicken is a resource because it can be used for food, it lays eggs that can be used for food, and its feathers can be used for pillows.

Day #3
What is a renewable resource? Give two examples.
A renewable resource is a resource that can be replaced in a person's lifetime. Possible examples: trees, crops, animals

What is an inexhaustible resource? Give two examples.
An inexhaustible resource is a resource that can be used repeatedly and not be used up. Possible examples: sun, air, water

Day #4
Where are most nonrenewable resources found?
Most nonrenewable resources are found under the surface of the Earth.

Should nonrenewable resources be used carefully? Explain.
Yes, nonrenewable resources should be used carefully, because once they are used, they are gone.

Assessment #34 — Week #34: Resources

Answer the questions.
1. Look at the picture. How is it a resource?
   Possible answers: A tree is a resource because people use it for many things, like paper, lumber for building houses, heating, cooking, and furniture.

2. Is it important to care for inexhaustible resources? Give an example in your explanation.
   Yes, it is important to care for inexhaustible resources because we need these things to live. Water is an inexhaustible resource, but if we do not keep eater clean, we cannot drink it and plants cannot use it to help them grow.

3. How does a lumber company make sure that a tree is a renewable resource?
   A lumber company will plant new trees to replace ones they cut down.

Fill in the circle next to the best answer:
4. What kind of resources are plants and animals?
   A) exhaustible ● **renewable** B) inexhaustible D) nonrenewable
5. Which is not an example of a nonrenewable resource?
   A) coal C) oil B) iron ● **water**

Published by Frank Schaffer Publications. Copyright protected.
0-7682-3523-5 Science 4 Today

Answer Key

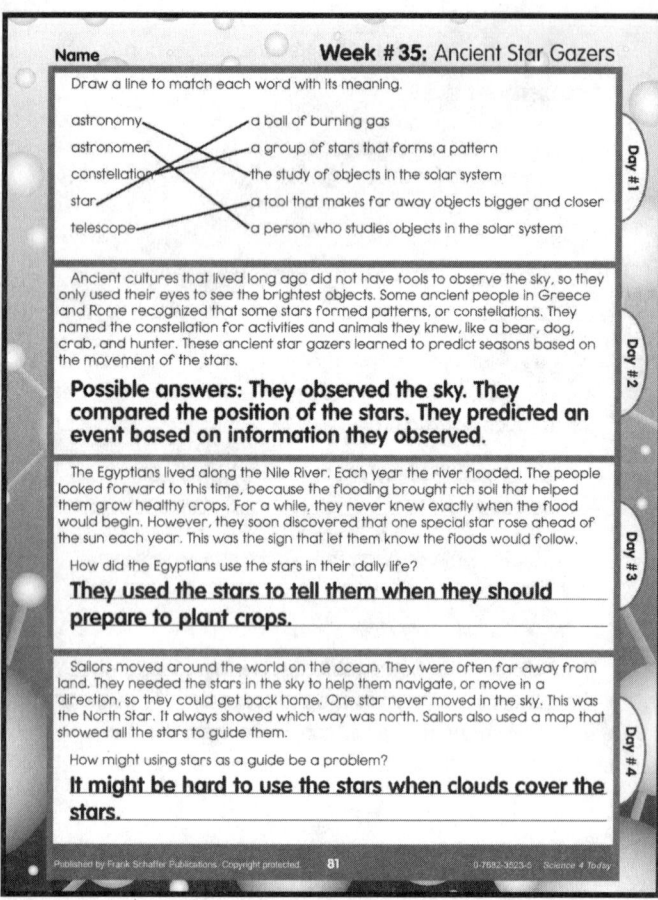

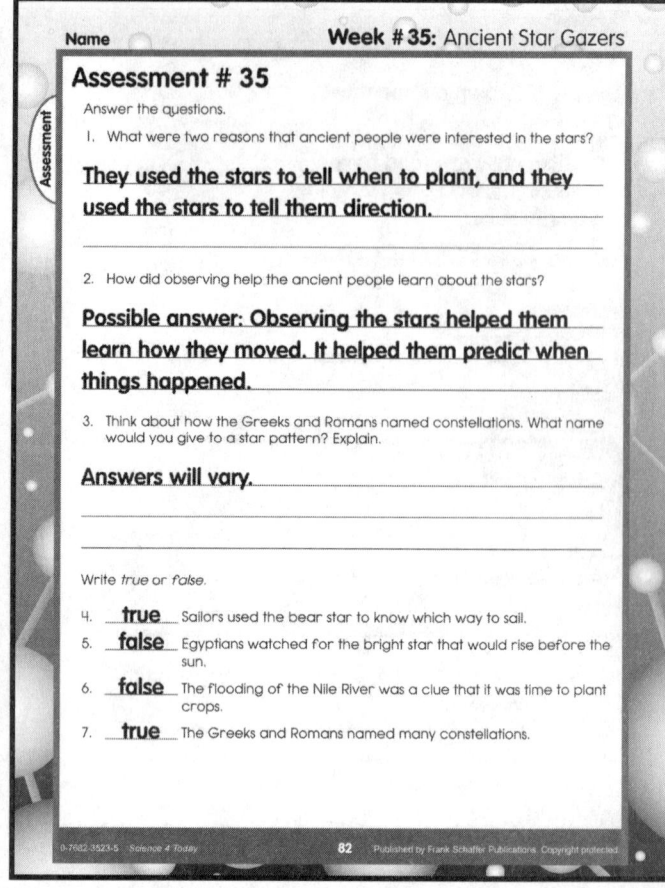

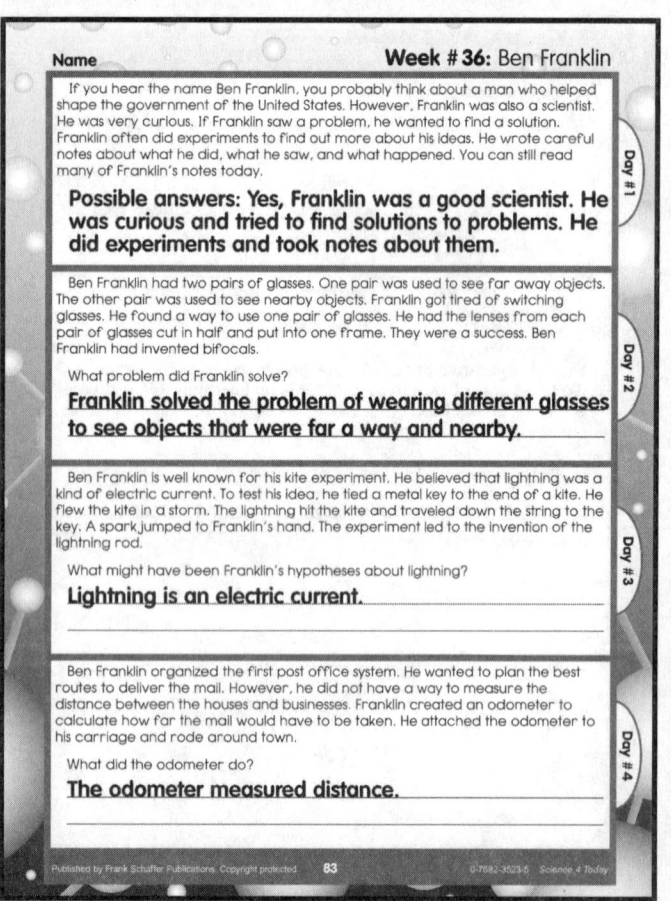

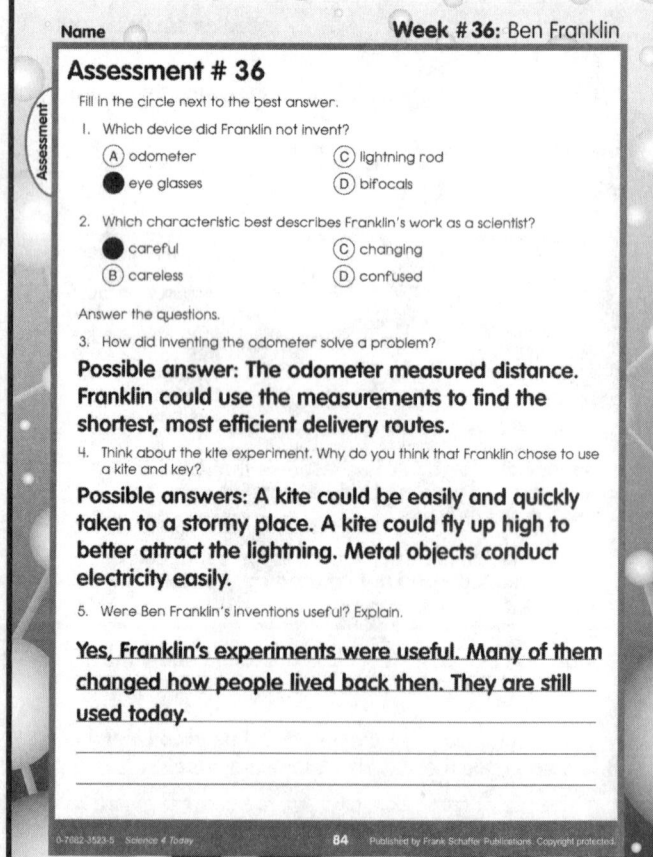

Week #35: Ancient Star Gazers

Day #1 — Draw a line to match each word with its meaning.
- astronomy → the study of objects in the solar system
- astronomer → a person who studies objects in the solar system
- constellation → a group of stars that forms a pattern
- star → a ball of burning gas
- telescope → a tool that makes far away objects bigger and closer

Day #2 — Ancient cultures that lived long ago did not have tools to observe the sky, so they only used their eyes to see the brightest objects. Some ancient people in Greece and Rome recognized that some stars formed patterns, or constellations. They named the constellation for activities and animals they knew, like a bear, dog, crab, and hunter. These ancient star gazers learned to predict seasons based on the movement of the stars.

Possible answers: They observed the sky. They compared the position of the stars. They predicted an event based on information they observed.

Day #3 — The Egyptians lived along the Nile River. Each year the river flooded. The people looked forward to this time, because the flooding brought rich soil that helped them grow healthy crops. For a while, they never knew exactly when the flood would begin. However, they soon discovered that one special star rose ahead of the sun each year. This was the sign that let them know the floods would follow.

How did the Egyptians use the stars in their daily life?
They used the stars to tell them when they should prepare to plant crops.

Day #4 — Sailors moved around the world on the ocean. They were often far away from land. They needed the stars in the sky to help them navigate, or move in a direction, so they could get back home. One star never moved in the sky. This was the North Star. It always showed which way was north. Sailors also used a map that showed all the stars to guide them.

How might using stars as a guide be a problem?
It might be hard to use the stars when clouds cover the stars.

Assessment #35

Answer the questions.

1. What were two reasons that ancient people were interested in the stars?
They used the stars to tell when to plant, and they used the stars to tell them direction.

2. How did observing help the ancient people learn about the stars?
Possible answer: Observing the stars helped them learn how they moved. It helped them predict when things happened.

3. Think about how the Greeks and Romans named constellations. What name would you give to a star pattern? Explain.
Answers will vary.

Write true or false.

4. **true** Sailors used the bear star to know which way to sail.
5. **false** Egyptians watched for the bright star that would rise before the sun.
6. **false** The flooding of the Nile River was a clue that it was time to plant crops.
7. **true** The Greeks and Romans named many constellations.

Week #36: Ben Franklin

Day #1 — If you hear the name Ben Franklin, you probably think about a man who helped shape the government of the United States. However, Franklin was also a scientist. He was very curious. If Franklin saw a problem, he wanted to find a solution. Franklin often did experiments to find out more about his ideas. He wrote careful notes about what he did, what he saw, and what happened. You can still read many of Franklin's notes today.

Possible answers: Yes, Franklin was a good scientist. He was curious and tried to find solutions to problems. He did experiments and took notes about them.

Day #2 — Ben Franklin had two pairs of glasses. One pair was used to see far away objects. The other pair was used to see nearby objects. Franklin got tired of switching glasses. He found a way to use one pair of glasses. He had the lenses from each pair of glasses cut in half and put into one frame. They were a success. Ben Franklin had invented bifocals.

What problem did Franklin solve?
Franklin solved the problem of wearing different glasses to see objects that were far away and nearby.

Day #3 — Ben Franklin is well known for his kite experiment. He believed that lightning was a kind of electric current. To test his idea, he tied a metal key to the end of a kite. He flew the kite in a storm. The lightning hit the kite and traveled down the string to the key. A spark jumped to Franklin's hand. The experiment led to the invention of the lightning rod.

What might have been Franklin's hypotheses about lightning?
Lightning is an electric current.

Day #4 — Ben Franklin organized the first post office system. He wanted to plan the best routes to deliver the mail. However, he did not have a way to measure the distance between the houses and businesses. Franklin created an odometer to calculate how far the mail would have to be taken. He attached the odometer to his carriage and rode around town.

What did the odometer do?
The odometer measured distance.

Assessment #36

Fill in the circle next to the best answer.

1. Which device did Franklin not invent?
   - A) odometer
   - ● B) eye glasses
   - C) lightning rod
   - D) bifocals

2. Which characteristic best describes Franklin's work as a scientist?
   - ● A) careful
   - B) careless
   - C) changing
   - D) confused

Answer the questions.

3. How did inventing the odometer solve a problem?
Possible answer: The odometer measured distance. Franklin could use the measurements to find the shortest, most efficient delivery routes.

4. Think about the kite experiment. Why do you think that Franklin chose to use a kite and key?
Possible answers: A kite could be easily and quickly taken to a stormy place. A kite could fly up high to better attract the lightning. Metal objects conduct electricity easily.

5. Were Ben Franklin's inventions useful? Explain.
Yes, Franklin's experiments were useful. Many of them changed how people lived back then. They are still used today.

Answer Key

Week #37: Famous Men Scientists — Day #1

What do shaving cream, mayonnaise, peanut butter, and cherry punch have in common? George Washington Carver! He was an inventor and scientist who worked with plants. By the 1900s, the soil in the south did not have many nutrients, and it did not hold water well. The cotton plants that had been grown for years had hurt the soil. Carver found that planting peanuts and sweet potatoes helped the soil.

How did planting peanuts and sweet potatoes help the soil?

The plants added nutrients to the soil so that it could help hold water.

Day #2

Thomas Edison had over 1,000 patents with his name on it. A patent gives a person or company who has an idea the right to be the only one who can use, make, or sell things with the idea. Edison spent many years learning about electricity and sound. One of his most well-known patents was received for the thread inside a light bulb. It made using lights in a house safe and useful. It was not too expensive, either.

Why would a scientist want to patent an idea?

Possible answer: A scientist would be able to make money using his idea.

Day #3

Putting lights in one house was easy. Yet Edison needed to find a way to get lights into every house. He needed to invent a system to link electricity to each house and business in a town. With more experiments, Edison invented parallel circuits, an underground conductor network, safety fuses, and off-on switches.

What problem did Edison have with lights?

Possible answer: Edison needed to use electricity to link the lights in houses and businesses to make it possible and affordable for everyone to have them.

Day #4

Thomas Edison may have invented an electric system, but it was Lewis Latimer who made improvements to the light bulb that really made it safe. Edison's light bulb only pushed into a socket. The bulb could easily fall out if the lamp tipped. Latimer invented a bottom that had threads. It could be screwed into the socket. Now the electric lamp was really safe.

Did adding screws to the bottom of the bulb make it safer? Explain.

Yes, the bulb was safer. The screw bottom held the bulb in the lamp. Now it could not fall out and break.

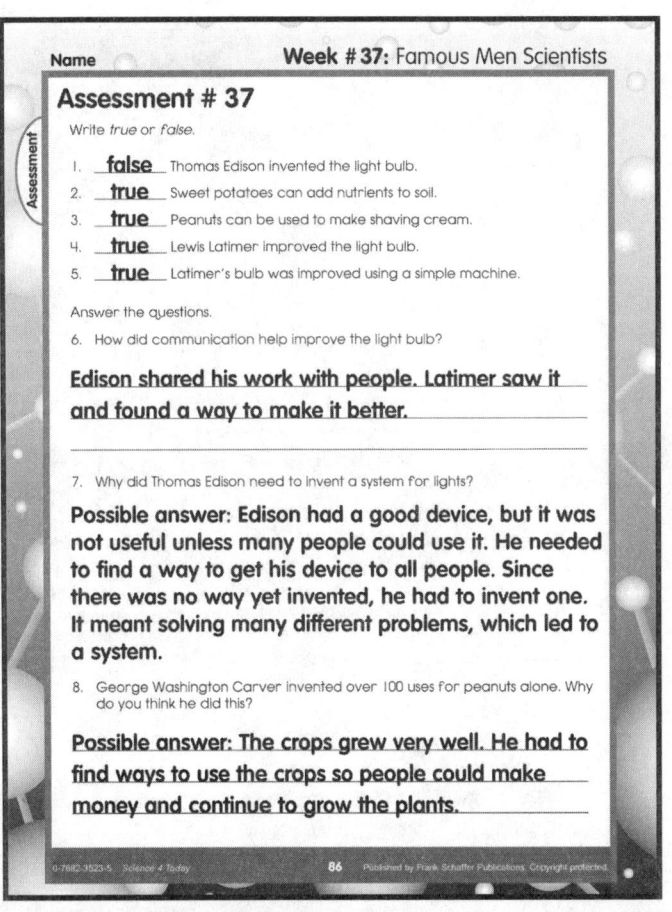

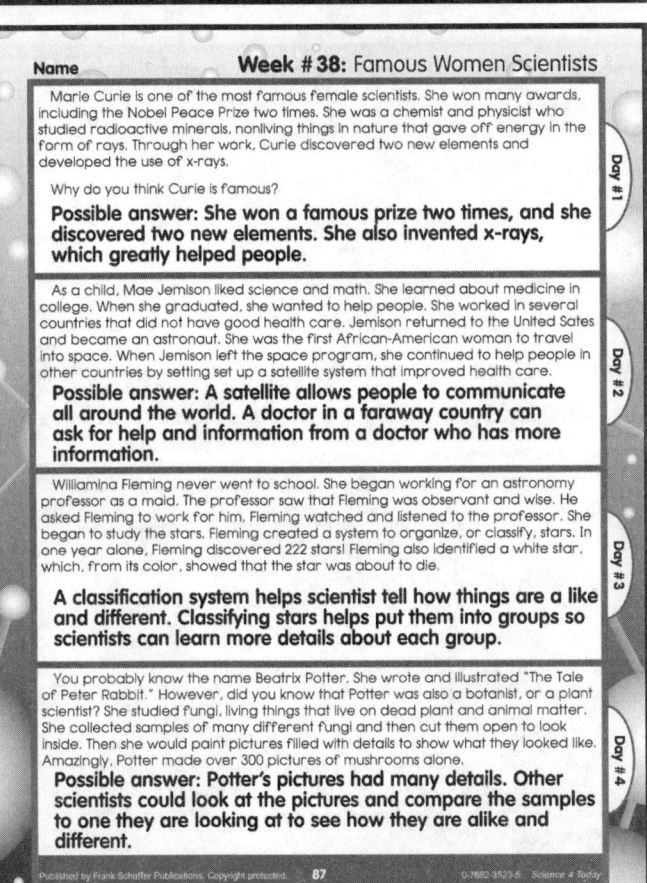

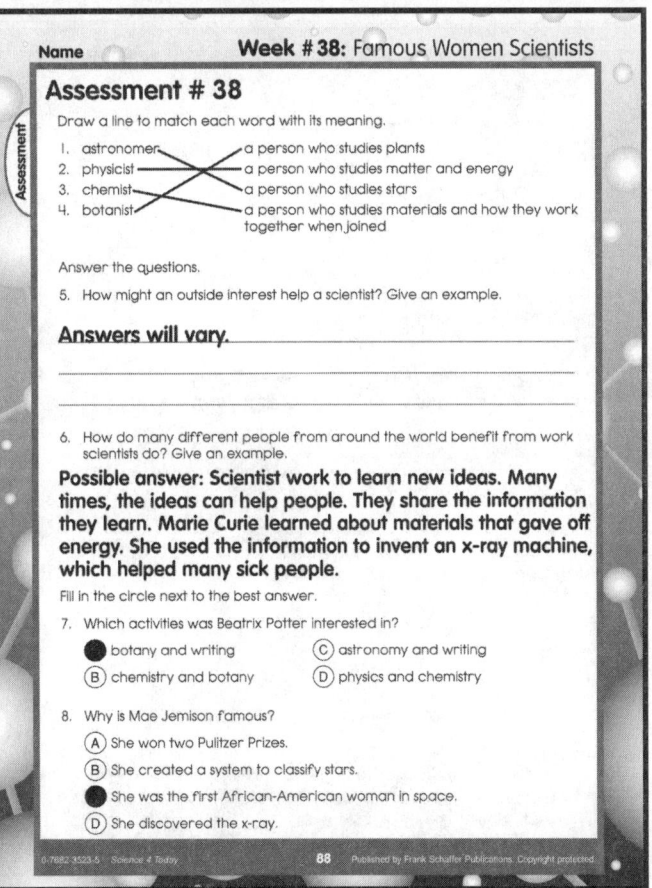

Week #37: Famous Men Scientists

Assessment # 37

Write true or false.

1. **false** Thomas Edison invented the light bulb.
2. **true** Sweet potatoes can add nutrients to soil.
3. **true** Peanuts can be used to make shaving cream.
4. **true** Lewis Latimer improved the light bulb.
5. **true** Latimer's bulb was improved using a simple machine.

Answer the questions.

6. How did communication help improve the light bulb?

Edison shared his work with people. Latimer saw it and found a way to make it better.

7. Why did Thomas Edison need to invent a system for lights?

Possible answer: Edison had a good device, but it was not useful unless many people could use it. He needed to find a way to get his device to all people. Since there was no way yet invented, he had to invent one. It meant solving many different problems, which led to a system.

8. George Washington Carver invented over 100 uses for peanuts alone. Why do you think he did this?

Possible answer: The crops grew very well. He had to find ways to use the crops so people could make money and continue to grow the plants.

Week #38: Famous Women Scientists — Day #1

Marie Curie is one of the most famous female scientists. She won many awards, including the Nobel Peace Prize two times. She was a chemist and physicist who studied radioactive minerals, nonliving things in nature that gave off energy in the form of rays. Through her work, Curie discovered two new elements and developed the use of x-rays.

Why do you think Curie is famous?

Possible answer: She won a famous prize two times, and she discovered two new elements. She also invented x-rays, which greatly helped people.

Day #2

As a child, Mae Jemison liked science and math. She learned about medicine in college. When she graduated, she wanted to help people. She worked in several countries that did not have good health care. Jemison returned to the United Sates and became an astronaut. She was the first African-American woman to travel into space. When Jemison left the space program, she continued to help people in other countries by setting set up a satellite system that improved health care.

Possible answer: A satellite allows people to communicate all around the world. A doctor in a faraway country can ask for help and information from a doctor who has more information.

Day #3

Williamina Fleming never went to school. She began working for an astronomy professor as a maid. The professor said that Fleming was observant and wise. He asked Fleming to work for him. Fleming watched and listened to the professor. She began to create a system to organize, or classify, stars. In one year alone, Fleming discovered 222 stars! Fleming also identified a white star, which, from its color, showed that the star was about to die.

A classification system helps scientist tell how things are a like and different. Classifying stars helps put them into groups so scientists can learn more details about each group.

Day #4

You probably know the name Beatrix Potter. She wrote and illustrated "The Tale of Peter Rabbit." However, did you know that Potter was also a botanist, or a plant scientist? She studied fungi, living things that live on dead plant and animal matter. She collected samples of many different fungi and then cut them open to look inside. Then she would paint pictures filled with details to show what they looked like. Amazingly, Potter made over 300 pictures of mushrooms alone.

Possible answer: Potter's pictures had many details. Other scientists could look at the pictures and compare the samples to one they are looking at to see how they are alike and different.

Week #38: Famous Women Scientists

Assessment # 38

Draw a line to match each word with its meaning.

1. astronomer — a person who studies stars
2. physicist — a person who studies matter and energy
3. chemist — a person who studies materials and how they work together when joined
4. botanist — a person who studies plants

Answer the questions.

5. How might an outside interest help a scientist? Give an example.

Answers will vary.

6. How do many different people from around the world benefit from work scientists do? Give an example.

Possible answer: Scientist work to learn new ideas. Many times, the ideas can help people. They share the information they learn. Marie Curie learned about materials that gave off energy. She used the information to invent an x-ray machine, which helped many sick people.

Fill in the circle next to the best answer.

7. Which activities was Beatrix Potter interested in?
- **● botany and writing**
- (B) chemistry and botany
- (C) astronomy and writing
- (D) physics and chemistry

8. Why is Mae Jemison famous?
- (A) She won two Pulitzer Prizes.
- (B) She created a system to classify stars.
- **● She was the first African-American woman in space.**
- (D) She discovered the x-ray.

Answer Key

Week #39: Fossils — Day #1

Draw a line to match each word with its meaning.

- fossil — something left over from a living thing that died long ago
- paleontology — the study of fossils
- mold — the shape of a living thing left as an imprint
- cast — the shape of a living thing made when mud or minerals fill a space
- dinosaur — a kind of animal that lived long ago

Day #2

Write numbers 1 through 5 to show how a fossil is made.

- **3** The soft parts rot.
- **2** Layers of small rocks, sand, and mud cover the organism.
- **1** The plant or animal dies.
- **5** A print of the organism remains in the rock.
- **4** The pressure of the layers of sediment forms rock.

Day #3

How do we know that dinosaurs lived on Earth?
There are fossils of organism parts, imprints of tracks, and casts of their bodies.

Why must a paleontologist work carefully when digging up fossils?
A paleontologist must work carefully so as not to lose or harm the fossils. The better and bigger the fossil, the more a scientist can learn.

Day #4

Professor Ray has two fossil teeth. One is long and pointed. The other is wide and flat. List two facts that Professor Ray can make about these teeth. Explain each fact.

Possible answers:

Fact 1: **The tooth that is sharp came from an animal that ate meat.**

Fact 2: **The tooth that is flat came from an animal that ate plants.**

Assessment #39

Answer the questions.

1. Why are most fossils found in sedimentary rocks?
Sedimentary rock is made of small pieces of rocks, sand, and mud. The small pieces take the shape of something and give more details.

2. What is the difference in a cast and a mold fossil?
In a mold, the parts of the organism were dissolved and left an imprint. In a cast, rock and mud fill the area that was dissolved to make a three-dimensional shape.

3. How might knowing about plants and animals living today help scientists learn about organisms that lived long ago?
Scientists can compare what they find with animals living today. If the parts are the same, they can make inferences and draw conclusions that the animals liked the same way.

4. Identify three tools a paleontologist needs to help dig fossils and explain their uses.

Tool 1: **Answers will vary.**

Tool 2: ____

Tool 3: ____

Week #40: Animal Conservation — Day #1

Draw a line to match each word to its meaning.

- conservation — to keep the living things on Earth safe
- extinct — every one of this kind of living thing has died
- endangered — there is only a small number of this living thing
- protected — a group of living things that is being kept safe by laws
- refuge — a place where the habitat of a living thing is kept safe

Day #2

Dinosaurs lived long ago. How do we know that these animals existed?
Possible answer: There are fossils of bones, teeth, and prints left behind in rocks.

Why do scientists think that all the dinosaurs died?
Possible answer: Changes in nature, such as climate and land changes, caused the dinosaurs to die.

Day #3

Bluebirds live in holes they find. The holes may be in trees or in fence posts. People started clearing the land to make roads, buildings, and farms. The bluebird population got smaller. Soon, the bird was added to the endangered list.

Think about what animals need. What did the bluebird not have?
Possible answers: The bluebird did not have a place to build a nest. It did not have food.

What did people do that caused the bluebird population to get smaller?
Possible answer: People changed the land.

Day #4

People worried that bluebirds would become extinct. They began to help the birds. People all over the United States built special boxes that the birds could live in. They nailed the boxes to trees beside meadows. Now the bluebird population is growing. The bluebirds have been removed from the endangered list in some states.

Possible answers: They put the bird on the endangered list so that it would be kept safe by laws. People built boxes that the bird could use to make a nest. People placed the boxes in a habitat where the birds had everything they needed to live.

Assessment #40

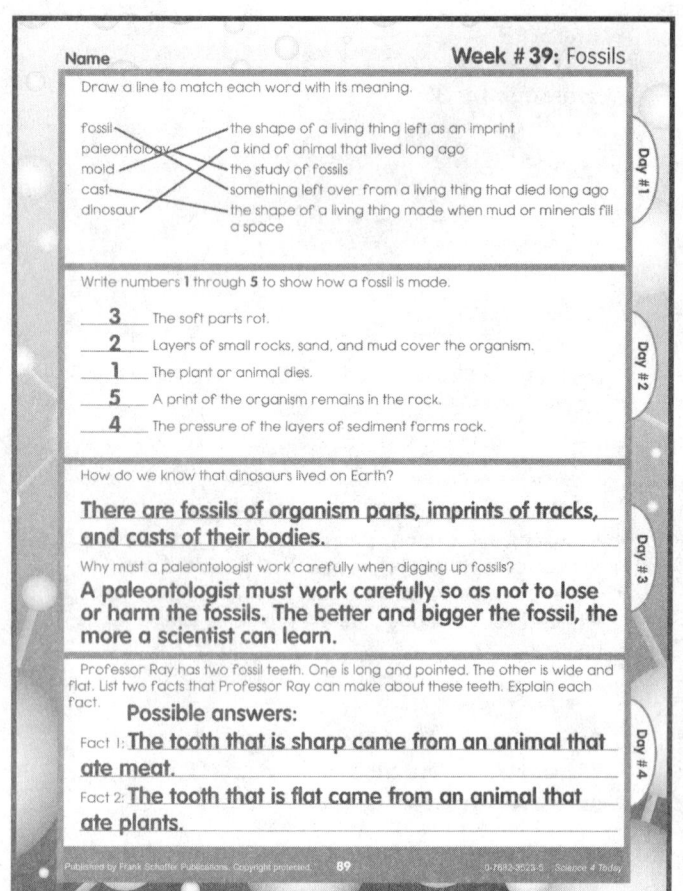

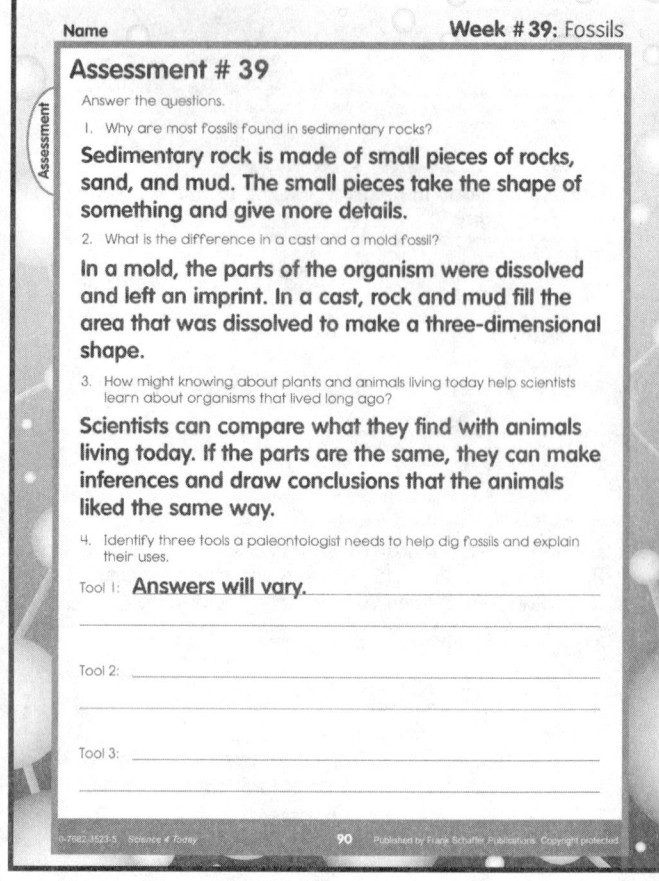

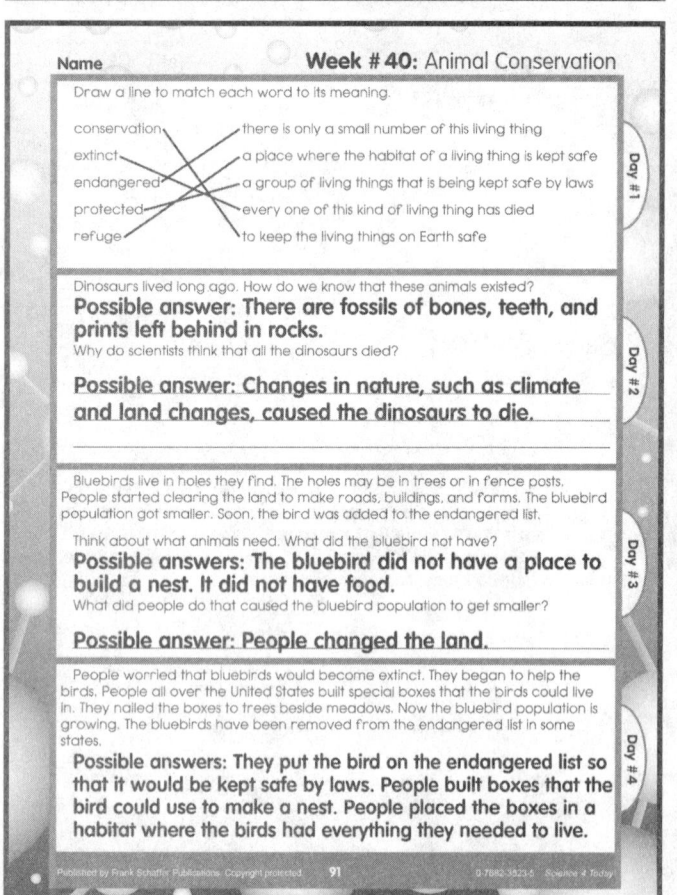

Read the selection. Then, answer the questions.

The bald eagle is the national symbol of the United States. At one time, many of these birds flew in the sky. Then, farmers began using chemicals to kill insects. Fish and other small animals ate the insects. The chemical was in those animals. The eagles then ate those animals. They too had the chemical in their bodies. They began laying eggs with thin shells. When the parents sat on the eggs, the eggs cracked. Few eagles were born. The bald eagle was added to the endangered list.

Scientists were puzzled. The chemicals were not used near the eagles. They worked to solve the problem. Now, those chemicals are not used. People are working to make sure the eagles have everything they need so their population will grow.

1. How did people harm the eagles?
They sprayed a harmful chemical.

2. How did knowing about a food chain help scientists discover the problem with eagles?
Possible answer: The chemicals were not used near eagles, but scientists realized the birds were getting the chemical in a food source.

3. How did people help the eagles?
Possible answers: People could not use the chemical anymore. Scientists worked to find a solution to the eagle problem.

4. Why is it important to understand the balance of nature?
Possible answer: Plants and animals are all connected. If something harms one living thing, it often affects another living thing. Animals or plants might die as a result. It is important to realize the connection to keep nature safe and balanced.